BAR INTERNATIONAL SERIES 3218 | 2025

Pre and Protohistoric Archaeology of Chunar, Mirzapur (Uttar Pradesh)

New research from Dantari Hill

Virag G. Sontakke, Sachin Kr. Tiwary and Dheeraj Sharma

Published in 2025 by
BAR Publishing, Oxford, UK

BAR International Series 3218

Pre and Protohistoric Archaeology of Chunar, Mirzapur (Uttar Pradesh)

ISBN 978 1 4073 6269 4 paperback
ISBN 978 1 4073 6270 0 e-format

DOI https://doi.org/10.30861/9781407362694

A catalogue record for this book is available from the British Library

© Authors and contributors 2025

COVER IMAGE: *Cairn type of megaliths at Dantari, Mirzapur (Uttar Pradesh).*

The Authors' moral rights under the 1988 UK Copyright,
Designs and Patents Act, are hereby expressly asserted.

All rights reserved. No part of this work may be copied, reproduced, stored, sold, distributed, scanned, saved in any form of digital format or transmitted in any form digitally, without the written permission of the Publisher.

Links to third party websites are provided by BAR Publishing in good faith and for information only. BAR Publishing disclaims any responsibility for the materials contained in any third party website referenced in this work.

BAR titles are available from:

BAR Publishing
122 Banbury Rd, Oxford, OX2 7BP, UK
info@barpublishing.com
www.barpublishing.com

Of Related Interest

Mayotte au temps des Califes (IXe - XIIe siècle)
Archéologie de l'Océan Indien à Ironi Be, Commune de Dembeni
Edited by Stéphane Pradines

BAR International Series S3199 | 2024

Holocene Foragers of North India
The Bioarchaeology of Mesolithic Damdama
John R. Lukacs, Jagannath Pal, with contributions by M.C. Gupta, V.D. Misra, Greg C. Nelson, and G. Robbins Schug

BAR International Series S2783 | 2016

Southeast Asia in the Ancient Indian Ocean World
Tom Hoogervorst

BAR International Series S2580 | 2013

The Prehistory of Kharagpur Hills South Bihar (India)
Manoj Kumar Singh

BAR International Series S2575 | 2013

Early Medieval Sanjan
Aspects and analysis
Sharad Rajaguru, Sushama Deo, Pramod Joglekar, Padmakar Prabhune, Vijay Sathe, Shivendra Kadgaonkar and Arati Deshpande-Mukherjee

BAR International Series S2509 | 2013

The Archaeology of the Hellenistic Far East: A Survey
Rachel Mairs

BAR International Series S2196 | 2011

Space, Time, Place
Third International Conference on Remote Sensing in Archaeology, 17th-21st August 2009, Tiruchirappalli, Tamil Nadu, India
Edited by Stefano Campana, Maurizio Forte and Claudia Liuzza

BAR International Series S2118 | 2010

Indigenous Archaeology in India
Prospects for an Archaeology of the Subaltern
Ajay Pratap

BAR International Series S1927 | 2009

Gurudakshina: Facets of Indian Archaeology
Essays presented to Prof. V. N. Misra
Edited by Alok Kumar Kanungo

BAR International Series S1433 | 2005

For more information, or to purchase these titles, please visit **www.barpublishing.com**

Acknowledgements

A special mention goes to Mahamana Pandit Madan Mohan Malviya, the visionary founder of Banaras Hindu University, whose legacy continues to shape and inspire our academic endeavours. Our deepest gratitude goes to the Archaeological Survey of India and Banaras Hindu University for fostering academic exploration and research, and for their continued funding support through agencies like the Indian Knowledge System and the Institute of Eminence (IoE) Grant of BHU.

We are indebted to the Archaeological Survey of India for granting permission to carry out the archaeological explorations in the Chunar area. We thank the Department of Ancient Indian History, Culture, and Archaeology at BHU for support. The Head of the Department's leadership and guidance have been instrumental, and we extend our heartfelt appreciation. Our gratitude also extends to the Dean of the Faculty of Arts for their support and encouragement. Our gratitude extends to the Vice-Chancellor of Banaras Hindu University, who has consistently inspired and motivated the younger generation to pursue their research passions.

We are grateful to the students of the post-graduation course who actively participated in the fieldwork, especially Abhishek Ranjan and Dhamma Ratana, for their tireless efforts in field documentation. Their dedication and passion were essential to the success of this project.

We would also like to thank the local villagers for their warmth and cooperation and Kabir Math, whose hospitality provided us with accommodation during our fieldwork. Their kindness in offering a place to stay and helping us with food was invaluable.

This research would not have been possible without the collective efforts and contributions of all those mentioned above. We are profoundly grateful to each one of you.

Authors
5th September, 2024

Contents

List of Figures	ix
List of Tables	xi
Foreword	xiii
References	xiv
Preface	xix

1. **Introduction**   1
   Virag G. Sontakke
   - Archaeological History   1
   - Aims and Objectives   4
   - Methodology of the work   5
     1. Megalithic Burials   5
     2. Microliths Collection   6
     3. Rock Art   6
     4. Habitation Sites   7
   - Scope of Work   7

2. **The Area**   9
   Virag G. Sontakke and Sachin Kr. Tiwary
   - Chunar   9
   - Dantari Hill   10
   - Environment Settings   10

3. **Megaliths of Dantari Hill: Typology, Placement and Locational Analysis**   17
   Virag G. Sontakke and Dheeraj Sharma
   - Methodology Adopted   18
   - Typology of Megaliths   19
     - a) Cairn: 20
     - b) Cist within cairn: 20
     - c) Menhir within cairn: 22
     - d) Menhir   22
   - Distribution of Megaliths at Dantari Hill   22
   - Quantitative Enquiry of Megaliths   23
   - Locational Analysis of the Megaliths   24
   - Megaliths and Human Destruction   25
   - The Construction Pattern of Megaliths   28
   - Artefacts and Key Features   28
   - Pottery   29

	Microliths	29
	Stone Disks	30
4.	**Microliths of Dantari Hill**	35
	Dheeraj Sharma, Sachin Kr. Tiwary and Pratik Pandey	
	Microlithic Technology in India	35
	Microliths	36
	Method for Collection of Microliths	36
	Analysis of Randomly Collected Microliths	38
	Analysis of Grid Collection Microliths	41
	Raw Material	43
	Discussion	45
5.	**Painted Rock Shelter of Dantari Hill**	47
	Sachin Kr. Tiwary, Dheeraj Sharma and Shubham Saurabh	
	Previous Work	47
	Location of the Shelter	48
	Methodology	48
	Micro-Documentation of the Execution and the Shelter	50
	Panel 1: War Scene and Faunal Cluster	50
	Panel 2: Diverse Imagery	52
	Panel 3: Complex Ceilings	55
	Panel 4: War and Geometric Scenes	56
	Panel 5: Anthropomorphic and Geometric Clusters	59
	Analysis	60
	Megalithic Burial Depiction	63
	Discussion	64
6.	**Archaeology of Chunar: Megaliths, Microliths and Rock Paintings**	65
	Dheeraj Sharma, Deepesh Singh and Virag G. Sontakke	
	Previous Work	65
	Megalithic Cemetery sites	67
	Maina Pahar (25.01388, 82.90767)	67
	Titwa Pahar (25.03027, 82.84526)	68
	Shakteshgarh (24.98043; 82.8356)	69
	Bahera (25.008278, 82.88998)	69
	Siddhanath-Ki-Dari (24.96899, 82.82216)	70
	Samudwa (25.01787, 82.85879)	71
	Rampur-38 (24.90267, 82.87464)	71
	Siyanhara (25.04938, 82.90897)	72
	Kharian Jangal-Mahal (25.04872, 82.93434)	72
	Kumhia (25.031088, 82.91288)	74
	Talaiya (24.90672, 82.83319)	74
	Semri-Sarso (24.9365, 82.82287)	74

Pokhraudh (24.90318, 82.81504)	74
Painted Rock Shelters	74
Siddhanath-Ki-Dari (24.96397, 82.82153)	75
Pahati Dari (24.97670, 82.74063)	75
Nanauti Dari (24.97326, 82.78279)	75
Bairahawa	75
Gobardaha (25.00008, 82.84346)	76
Microlithic Sites	76
Habitation Sites	76
Baheri (25.02013, 82.9056)	76
Banimilia (25.00809, 82.9248)	77
Bahera (25.01092, 82.89442)	79
Stone Quarry Sites	84
7. Conclusion	**87**
Virag G. Sontakke, Sachin Kr. Tiwary and Dheeraj Sharma	
Bibliography	**93**

List of Figures

Fig. 2.1. Location map of Dantari Hill, Mirzapur District, Uttar Pradesh	11
Fig. 2.2. Lithology map of Mirzapur District, Uttar Pradesh	12
Fig. 2.3. Elevation map of Mirzapur District, Uttar Pradesh	14
Fig. 2.4. Average rainfall map of Mirzapur District, Uttar Pradesh	15
Fig. 3.1. Micro-documentation of megalithic burial at Dantari Hill	19
Fig. 3.2. Distribution of megalithic burials at Dantari Hill	20
Fig. 3.3. Cairn type of megalith at Dantari Hill	21
Fig. 3.4. Cist within cairn type of megalith at Dantari Hill	21
Fig. 3.5. Menhir within cairn type of megalith at Dantari Hill	22
Fig. 3.6. Cluster-wise distributions of the megaliths at Dantari Hill	23
Fig. 3.7. Type-wise distributions of the megaliths at Dantari Hill	24
Fig. 3.8. The placement of megaliths in different areas of the Dantari Hill	24
Fig. 3.9. Size-wise distributions of the megaliths at Dantari Hill	25
Fig. 3.10. Distribution of the megaliths according to the elevation of Dantari Hill	25
Fig. 3.11. Vandalised megalith at Dantari Hill	26
Fig. 3.12: Destruction of megalith showing the construction pattern	27
Fig. 3.13. The present quantity of the megaliths according to their conditions	27
Fig. 3.14. Ceramics recovered from megalithic burials at Dantari Hill	28
Fig. 3.15. Stone disks recovered from the top of megalithic burials	29

Fig. 4.1. General view of grids and spatial distribution of lithic assemblages   37

Fig. 4.2. A. General view of the grid layout, B. Close-up view of the grid, C. Core and microliths   37

Fig. 4.3. Random collection of microliths from megalithic burials   38

Fig. 4.4. Randomly collected artefacts from Dantari Hill   38

Fig. 4.5. Blade and microblades recovered from the megalithic clusters of Dantari Hill   39

Fig. 4.6.a. Metrical values of width for microblades (A) and cores (B) at Dantari Hill   40

Fig. 4.6.b. Metrical values of length for microblades (A) and cores (B) at Dantari Hill   40

Fig. 4.7. Distribution of artefacts collected from the grid pattern in each block   42

Fig. 4.8. Microblade distribution order, Dantari Hill   42

Fig. 4.9. Type of flakes in lithic assemblages of Dantari Hill   43

Fig. 4.10. Distribution of debitage in each block   43

Fig. 4.11. Preference of raw material at Dantari Hill   44

Fig. 4.12. Collected microlithic artefacts from Dantari Hill   45

Fig. 5.1. Location map of painted rock shelter   49

Fig. 5.2. Line drawing of the five different panels and clusters   49

Fig. 5.3. General view of the shelter along with the Jargo dam   50

Fig. 5.4. Horse riders with weapons in the panel 1.1 (D-Stretch)   51

Fig. 5.5. Human figure along with animal showing domestication scene (D-Stretch)   54

Fig. 5.6: General view of the panel 4.1. (D-Stretch)   57

Fig. 5.7. Warrior scene with bows, arrows, sword and shield of panel 4.1.   58

Fig. 5.8. General and close view (D-Stretch) of the panel 5 in the rectangular shape   59

Fig. 5.9. Panel-wise distribution of the rock painting, Dantari Hill   60

Fig. 5.10. Colour-wise distribution of the rock painting, Dantari Hill   61

List of Figures

Fig. 5.11. Orientation-wise distribution of the rock painting, Dantari Hill	61
Fig. 5.12. Rock painting executed on different heights (in cm) Dantari Hill	62
Fig. 5.13. Scene-wise distribution of the rock painting, Dantari Hill	62
Fig. 5.14. Megalithic burial depiction at Dantari Hill	63
Fig. 6.1: Distribution of archaeological sites in Chunar, Mirzapur, Uttar Pradesh	66
Fig.6.2. Distribution of megalithic burials at Maina Pahar	68
Fig. 6.3. Size variations of megaliths at Maina Pahar	68
Fig.6.4. Distribution of megalithic burials at Titwa Pahar	69
Fig.6.5. Size variations of megalithic burials at Titwa Pahar	69
Fig. 6.6. Different types of megaliths at Shakteshgarh	70
Fig. 6.7. Size variations of megalithic burials at Shakteshgarh	70
Fig.6.8. Different types of megaliths documented in Bahera	71
Fig. 6.9. Size variations of megaliths at Bahera	71
Fig. 6.10. Different types of megaliths at Siddhanath-Ki-Dari	72
Fig.6.11. Different types of megaliths at Samudwa	72
Fig. 6.12. Size variations of megaliths at Samudwa	73
Fig. 6.13. Different types of megalithic burials at Rampur-38	73
Fig. 6.14. Different sizes of megaliths at Rampur-38	73
Fig. 6.15. General view of habitation mound at Baheri	77
Fig. 6.16. Cross transect survey-layout of habitation mound at Baheri	78
Fig. 6.17. General view of habitation mound at Banimilia	79
Fig. 6.18. Cross transect survey layout of habitation mound at Banimilia	80
Fig. 6.19. Potsherds recovered from habitation mound at Banimilia	81
Fig. 6.20. Potsherds and associated findings recovered from habitation mound at Banimilia	82
Fig. 6.21. General view of habitation deposit at Bahera	82

Fig. 6.22. Cross transect survey layout of habitation mound at Bahera — 83

Fig. 6.23. Potsherds recovered from habitation mound at Banimilia — 84

Fig. 7.1. Typological distribution of megaliths in Chunar, Mirzapur, Uttar Pradesh — 90

List of Tables

Table 3.1. List of megalithic sites of the Mirzapur district, Uttar Pradesh   31

Table 4.1. Statistics of artifacts in the Dantari grid collection   41

Foreword

The writing of this foreword brings me back to the days of the 'Village-to-Village Survey' conducted in the Rajgarh block (Tehsil Chunar, dist. Mirzapur) in 1979. As if I am once again roaming around in that area's delightful uplands and sloping red-yellow Vindhyan terrain comprising valleys, forests full of fragmented mahua and palash with flaming red flowers, and waterfalls. During that exploration a good number of sites containing microliths, painted rock-shelters, polished lithic celts, megaliths, habitation sites comprising black-slipped and NBP potsherds, etc. were located and reported (Singh: BMA, Vols. 17-18: 91-92; IAR 1978-79: 24; Tewari 1997: 51-57). At that time, most of the megaliths were found disturbed by the locals to find treasure believed to be buried under them. However, many of them were well preserved and intact.

Five megaliths and a habitation site, located to the north-east of Rajgarh block in the 'Jangal Mahal' area, between Banimalia and Bahera villages, were subjected to archaeological excavations by P.C. Pant of the BHU during the early sixties of the last century (IAR 1962-63: 38-39). These excavations revealed mainly ill-fired dull red ware occasionally coated with red slip, along with black-slipped and black-and-red wares (no NBPW potsherd was found), both from the megaliths as well as the habitation site. Dantari Hill, which is explicitly discussed in the book under consideration (*Pre and Protohistoric Archaeology of Chunar, Mirzapur (Uttar Pradesh): New research from Dantari Hill*), is also located in the same area between the above-mentioned Banimilia and Bahera villages.

Notably, Carlleyle had reported painted rock-shelters near Sohagi Ghat in districts Mirzapur and Rewa during 1867-68. Microliths, rubbed and raw hematite pieces, and potsherds revealed in the excavations, carried out within the painted rock shelters and nearby burial mounds, were placed in Stone Age by him. He also suggested probable relations between the inhabitants of cave-shelters and those related with the burial mounds (Carlleyle 1883: 49; Smith 1906: 185-195). On the other hand, considering the adverse effects of human and natural factors causing rock-paintings' deterioration and destruction, Cockburn emphasized that "their examination ought to be taken up as speedily as possible." (Cockburn 1899: 96-97).

Subsequently, after a gap of more than eight decades, human burials were revealed in the excavations conducted, by the Allahabad University, in the Baghai Khor (IAR 1962-63: 37) and Lekhahiya (IAR 1963-64: 39) rock shelters. Based on radiocarbon dates these burials are dated from about 6, 420 + 75 BC; 6, 050 + 75 BC (Misra, V.N. 2002: 63, 67; Misra, V.D. 2002: 456).

Ancient remains found in Jangal Mahal and near-by surroundings provide evidence of human activities and habitation from the prehistoric period to the modern day. Considering the presence of black-slip and black-and-red wares and the absence of NBPW in the habitation deposits as well as in the megaliths excavated at Banimilia–Bahera, the lower limit for the beginning of megalithic construction in this area may be suggested around mid-second millennium BC, if not earlier. This tradition must have continued during the subsequent period. However, the antiquity of its upper limit is yet to be ascertained.

Given the above background, this book fully fulfills the task of examination, analysis and micro-documentation of all the sites comprising microlith-assemblages, painted rock-shelters and megaliths of 'Dantari Hill'. Apart from that earlier archaeological research carried out in dist. Mirzapur and other areas are also discussed to situate them in a larger context. This type of detailed documentation and study has become necessary due to the increasing human intervention in heritage sites with the ever-growing demographic pressure. This remarkable work also sets a model for similar documentation of other heritage sites. The efforts put in this regard, by the learned authors of this book, are highly appreciable. I hope they will continue further research at 'Dantari Hill' and excavate some of the potential megaliths and other sites to understand the evolution, development and other aspects of the respective human cultures from the prehistoric times onwards. I extend my heartfelt best wishes for their success.

Rakesh Tewari
C-1/173, Sector G, Jankipuram,   Date: 12.10.2024
Lucknow (U.P.), India – 226 021

References

Carlleyle, A.C.L. 1883 (for Feb. 1883), Notes on lately discovered sepulchral mounds, cairns, caves, cave-paintings, and stone implements, *Proceedings of the Asiatic Society of Bengal*, Edited by The Honorary Secretary, January-December 1983, Calcutta, Printed by J.W. Thomas, Baptist Mission Press, and Published by the Asiatic Society, 57 Park Street, 1884. p. 49.)

Cockburn, J. 1899. Cave Drawings in the Kaimur Range, North West Provinces, *The Journal of the Royal Asiatic Society of Great Britain and Ireland (January)*: pp. 88-97.

Indian Archaeology: A Review 1962-63, 1978-79. Archaeological Survey of India.

Indian Archaeology: A Review 1963-64, 1978-79. Archaeological Survey of India.

Misra, V.D. 2002. Origin, Chronology and Transformation of the Mesolithic Culture in India, in VD Misra and J.N.Pal (eds.) *Mesolithic India*: pp. 447-464. Allahabad: Department of Ancient History, Culture & Archaeology, University of Allahabad.

Misra, V.N. 2002. Mesolithic Culture India: Kea Note, in V.D. Misra and J..N. Pal (eds.) *Mesolithic India*: pp. 1-46. Allahabad: Department of Ancient History, Culture & Archaeology, University of Allahabad.

Singh, R.C. - 'Survey', *Bulletin of Museums and Archaeology, U.P. Lucknow* (BMA), Vols. 17 and 18, June and Dec. 1976, pp. 90-92.

Smith, V. A. 1906. Pygmy Flints, T*he Indian Antiquary, A Journal of Oriental Research in Archaeology, Epigraphy, Ethnology, Geography, History, Folklores, Languages, Literature, Numismatics, Philosophy, Religion, &c, &c*, Vol. XXXV, pp. 185-195.

Tewari, R. 1997. Gram stariya Sarvekshan: Vikas Khand Rajgarh, Jila Mirzapur [in Hindi], *Pragdhara No. 7:* pp. 51-57.

Preface

The title of this book, *Pre and Protohistoric Archaeology of Chunar, Mirzapur, (Uttar Pradesh) New Research from Dantari Hill*, evokes an air of mystery and anticipation. It invites the reader to explore an ancient land steeped in historical and archaeological significance. Dantari Hill, of Kaimur range largely unexplored due to its challenging terrain and remote location, offers clues to a long-forgotten world. Beneath its rugged exterior lies a wealth of historical treasures waiting to be uncovered. Dheeraj Sharma discovered the site while exploring the megalithic distribution of the Vindhya. His keen eye and passion for unearthing the past revealed significant findings, including ancient megalithic structures, rock art, and microlithic sites. The area, long overlooked due to its difficult accessibility, was found to contain rich archaeological deposits, making it a key study area. While the harsh landscape deterred researchers, it also preserved the area's archaeological integrity. The challenge of studying megaliths, damaged by natural and human forces, was a primary reason for selecting this area for this research.

The exploration of the area was extensive; we documented, analysed, and classified the scattered remains of microliths, megaliths, and rock art into seven chapters. Each chapter of this book has been meticulously crafted to reflect the breadth and depth of our research. *Chapter 1: Introduction* introduces the geographical and archaeological significance of the Mirzapur district in southeastern Uttar Pradesh. It highlights the area's continuous human presence since prehistoric times and emphasises its rich cultural heritage, making it a vital subject for archaeological research. The chapter also provides an overview of past investigations by prominent scholars like Sir Alexander Cunningham, clarifying why this region holds historical and cultural importance. *Chapter 2: The Area* gives a detailed geographical description of the Mirzapur district and the Chunar region. Over millennia, the area's landscape, fertile plains, hills, and rich natural resources attracted human settlement. This geographical understanding is key to interpreting the cultural artefacts found in the region. Special attention is paid to Dantari Hill, where significant archaeological findings were made, linking human activity to the area's unique geological features. *Chapter 3: Megaliths of Dantari Hill: Typology Placement and Locational Analysis* focuses on the megalithic structures found on Dantari Hill. It explores these burial sites' typology, placement, and locational analysis. The chapter underscores the importance of megalithic burials as a window into understanding ancient societies' burial practices and social structures. It also examines the threats these sites face from natural erosion and human activities such as quarrying, highlighting the urgency of their documentation and preservation. *Chapter 4: Microliths of Dantari Hill* discusses the discovery of microlithic tools at Dantari Hill, shedding light on the technological capabilities of prehistoric communities. The chapter thoroughly examines the types of tools, their production techniques, and the significance of microliths in understanding ancient people's daily lives and survival strategies. The spatial distribution of these artefacts across different burial sites also provides clues about these tools' social and ceremonial roles. *Chapter 5: Painted Rock Shelter of Dantari Hill* explores the rock art found in the shelters of Dantari Hill. The rock paintings, which depict scenes from daily life, hunting, and rituals, offer a glimpse into the symbolic world of early human societies. The chapter documents the detailed process of recording these paintings and analyses the stylistic and thematic elements that connect them to broader traditions in Indian rock art. *Chapter 6: Archaeology of Chunar: Megaliths, Microliths, and Rock Paintings* focused on a broader survey of the Chunar region is presented, including the examination of megalithic cemeteries, microlithic tools, and rock paintings. The chapter ties together the archaeological findings from different periods and locations, comprehensively understanding the region's historical and cultural landscape. This holistic approach allows the reader to grasp different cultural practices' interconnectedness over time. *Chapter 7: Conclusion* synthesises the findings from all the previous chapters, emphasising the significance of Dantari Hill and Chunar in the broader context of prehistoric and protohistoric archaeology in India. It reflects on the region's ancient inhabitants' technological, social, and cultural contributions and offers insights into future research directions. These descriptions will enrich the preface by highlighting the importance of each chapter, ensuring readers understand the book's value and contribution to Indian archaeology.

By focusing on a relatively neglected area, this book enriches the overall understanding of Indian archaeology. It adds to the growing body of work that aims to map the prehistory and proto-history of India, particularly concerning the larger South Asian context. The book covers a wide range of archaeological elements, from megalithic structures to rock art and microlithic tools, offering a holistic view of the cultural and technological evolution of ancient communities in this region. It brings together multiple aspects of archaeology-burial practices, rock art, microlithic tools, and landscape study-allowing for a broader understanding of the ancient inhabitants' lifestyles.

This book significantly contributes to archaeology, offering new insights into the pre-and protohistoric periods of the Chunar and Mirzapur regions. Its comprehensive documentation of megalithic, microlithic, and rock art sites provides a detailed understanding of this area's cultural and historical developments. The interdisciplinary approach in this research, combining archaeology, geology, and anthropology, ensures that the findings are well-rounded and thoroughly examined. This book is essential for anyone interested in South Asian archaeology, particularly those focused on prehistoric and protohistoric studies. Researchers and students alike will find it a valuable resource for understanding the cultural landscape of Chunar and Dantari Hill. Furthermore, the book highlights the importance of preserving these ancient sites for future generations, emphasising the need for ongoing research and conservation efforts. This work serves as a testament to the rich and diverse heritage of the Chunar region, encouraging further exploration and study of its hidden treasures.

Authors
5th September, 2024

Chapter 1
Introduction

Virag G. Sontakke

Mirzapur, located in southeastern Uttar Pradesh, is a region of considerable archaeological and historical significance. Situated along the southern bank of the Ganges River, this area has witnessed a continuous human presence since prehistoric times. Its rich and diverse cultural heritage is evident in the numerous archaeological remains scattered throughout the region. These remnants offer invaluable insights into the lives, practices, and advancements of ancient communities that once flourished here. The area falls within the Vindhyachal region, and its geophysical diversity has ensured its activity since ancient times. Archaeological research in the region affirms its potential, and the material remains gathered from excavations and explorations reveal continued occupation from the prehistoric to the medieval period.

Archaeological History

Archaeological investigation in Mirzapur district has a limited history. Sir Alexander Cunningham was the first to mark this region on the archaeological map. During his exploration in 1861-62, he identified several cairns and stone circles in a wide area of Mirzapur (Cunningham 1871:30-31). After Cunningham, Le Mesurier reported megalithic monuments in the hilly area of Chunar in 1867. He documented around a hundred cairns (tumuli) or stone barrows, each containing a cist or kist (Mesurier 1867: 164-166). This year also marked an important milestone for rock art in India. A.C.L. Carlleyle found the country's first painted rock shelter in this region in 1867; however, he didn't publish his findings until 1883. Apart from painted rock shelters, Carlleyle also reported sepulchral mounds, cairns and stone implements (Carlleyle 1883: 49-55). In the late 19th century, James Cockburn was also active in this area. He not only discovered painted rock shelters in the Mirzapur district but also provided detailed reports about his findings (Cockburn 1883a: 56-64, 1883b: 125-126; 1884a: 141-143,1884b: 140-141; 1888: 57-65; 1889: 89-97).

In addition to reporting archaeological findings, some colonial officers also conducted excavations. Rivett Carnac and John

Cockburn opened two megaliths in Mirzapur. One of the excavated megaliths was a stone circle with a diameter of twelve feet. The excavation revealed a complete skeleton of a six-foot-tall adult male at a depth of six or eight feet. The skeleton was placed on a stone slab in a north-south direction. Burial goods included glazed pottery and similar ceramics in each corner, as well as a long, narrow, lachrymal vase of green glass about seven inches long. Excavations of the second megalith yielded no skeletal remains but uncovered two stone hammers and flint flakes, which they considered belonging to the Neolithic period (Brockman 1911: 198).

At the beginning of the 20th century, several independent Indian scholars were active in Mirzapur. In 1918, K.N. Dikshit reported some painted rock shelters (Ghosh 1932:15). In 1931, M. Ghosh made copies of the known rock paintings in Mirzapur (Ghosh 1932:15-20). This marked a new beginning in the documentation of rock paintings. However, the other areas of the district lacked representation during this period.

After independence, the region witnessed a series of archaeological activities from several institutions. The systematic exploratory approach brought to light numerous megalithic cemeteries, painted rock shelters, stone tools, and habitation mounds spread throughout the district. Allahabad University reported many painted rock shelters, including Sahbaiya, Bediya, Lalbediya, Baga, Baghai Khor, Khari Pahadi, and Mini Baba, among others (IAR 1956-57: 11-14; IAR 1962-63: 31-32; IAR 1963-64: 39, 51-52; IAR 1969-70: 38). In 1962-63, Allahabad University conducted a megalithic burial excavation at Kakoria, in Chakia sub-division of Chandauli district, in the adjacent region of Mirzapur district. This was the first megalithic excavation in the area to be carried out after independence (IAR 1962-63: 39-41). At the same time, Banaras Hindu University was also involved in megalithic research. In 1962, they excavated five different types of megaliths in the villages of Banimilia Bahera in the Jangal Mahal area of Mirzapur. These megaliths yielded a few bone fragments, microliths, and ceramics of dull red ware, red ware, black slipped ware and black-and-red ware. The habitation deposits revealed pottery similar to that found in the megaliths (IAR 1962-63: 38-39).

In 1963-1964, the University of Allahabad conducted excavations of rock shelters at Lekhahia in the district of Mirzapur. This excavation uncovered seventeen skeletons from the rock shelters at Lekhahia (IAR 1963-64: 51-52). In the 1970s, the University of Allahabad reported numerous Chalcolithic sites on the northern edges of the

Vindhyan range. Many megalithic sites have been discovered in the Belan Valley and surrounding regions of the northeastern Vindhyas (IAR 1969-70: 36-38). In the years 1975-76, P.C. Pant and Vidula Jayaswal examined the river's cliff section, as well as the valleys of Belan and Seoti in the districts of Allahabad and Mirzapur. The exploration also revealed several rock shelters producing microliths (IAR 1975-76: 43-44). In the year 1977-78, G.R. Sharma and his team from Allahabad University conducted exploration in the Mirzapur district and reported prehistoric sites ranging from the Lower Palaeolithic to the Mesolithic period (IAR 1977-78: 56-57). Simultaneously, R.C. Singh of the Department of Archaeology, Government of Uttar Pradesh, help explore many rock shelters and ancient sites at Jafarabad, Patraura, and Sherwan in the Mirzapur district (IAR 1977-78: 58). In 1979-80, Allahabad University identified a major megalithic burial pocket in the valley of Adwa in Mirzapur. G.R. Sharma excavated megalithic sites at Magha in Mirzapur and the adjacent regions of Amahata and Munhai situated in the Rewa district of Madhya Pradesh (Misra et *al.* 2014:342-275). P. C. Pant and Vidula Jayaswal inferred the archaeological exploration in the area and brought to light fourteen megaliths on the hillside near Chunar in Chhilahina village (IAR 1990-91:75). Rakesh Tewari discovered megalithic monuments in Kankaira Pahar, Jaugarh, and Sakteshgarh in the extensive research (Tewari 1997: 51-58).

In addition to prehistoric and protohistoric remains, Mirzapur also contains historic remains. Several sites included pottery types such as NBPW, black slipped ware, red ware, black ware, black-and-red ware, and grey ware, spanning from the 6th century BCE to the Medieval period (Tewari 1997: 51-58; 1999: 163-223). In 1998-99, Banaras Hindu University conducted excavations at Agiabir in Mirzapur District. This ancient settlement, situated on the left bank of the Ganga, yielded evidence spanning from the Neolithic to the Medieval period (Singh and Singh 2004: 1-94, Singh and Shankar 2018: 95-129).

Moreover, Mirzapur has been a significant source of sandstone since ancient times. P.C. Pant and Vidula Jayaswal traced an ancient quarry site of the Mauryan period (Pant and Jayaswal 1990: 49-52). They identified the quarry site at Badagaon near the Chunar block in Mirzapur, where the Ashokan pillars were carved (Jayaswal 1998). Additionally, many scholars have explored this region, uncovering several archaeological sites (Kumar 2022; Pratap 2016: 54-89; Tewari 1990: 1-59). These findings highlight Mirzapur's rich archaeological heritage and underscore its importance in understanding ancient history.

Initially, our investigation concentrated solely on Dantari Hill. However, as the study progressed, we noticed the archaeological potential in the surrounding regions of Chunar. This led to expanding our research to include the Chunar area for a more comprehensive understanding of this region's cultural and historical developments. As we explored deeper, we broadened our focus from the megaliths to microliths and rock paintings sites. Chunar is situated close to the Varanasi and comprises Ganga alluvium and Vindhyan outcrop in north and south, respectively. This area was relatively less explored, but owing potential for archaeological research, exploration carried out in this area was fruitful and revealed exciting facets of the cultural wealth of the region. In Chunar, the exploration revealed several microlithic sites, rock shelters, megalithic cemeteries, and habitation deposits. The exploration uncovered an archaeological potential site known as Dantari Hill in the southwest area of Chunar. Here, evidence of various cultural activities, such as numerous megalithic burials, several microliths, painted rock shelters, and post-medieval inscriptions has been found. This cultural evidence makes Dantari Hill a prominent centre in the Chunar. The present research is a result of a detailed investigation of Chunar and Dantari Hill aimed to identifying and understanding the cultural progress of the area and its relationship.

Aims and Objectives

- This research explores the distribution of prehistoric and protohistoric sites in Chunar, Mirzapur district. This includes identifying the evidence of human presence, tracing the development of settlements, and understanding the factors influencing human habitations.
- To explore megalithic cemetery sites to understand megalithic typology and its distribution through detailed documentation.
- The exposed megalithic burials attract natives for hidden treasures. This belief in treasure has led to significant portions of the megalithic burials being dug up and destroyed. Additionally, long-term quarrying activities have further contributed to the damage and destruction of these burials. This research seeks to document these megalithic burials before their destruction.
- Identify the rock painting sites and trade out their significance through proper investigations. Natural factors are causing the rock paintings to fade over time. To preserve these paintings before they vanish entirely, micro-documentation is necessary.
- The Chunar area contains several scattered microlithic sites. The disturbed megalithic burials revealed an association between

Introduction

microliths and megalithic monuments. This work aims to understand microliths, focusing on their distribution, material, production techniques, placement, and relationship with megalithic burials.
- Other aim is to assess cultural significance of Dantari Hill. In this, the importance of Dantari Hill will be evaluated in the broader context by exploring the complete area of Dantari, adjoining region connections, and other contemporary sites to understand its role in the cultural and historical landscape.
- This study investigates the environmental context of prehistoric and protohistoric life in Chunar. This involves studying the climate, vegetation, and resources available to ancient people in the region.
- To create awareness about archaeological heritage of Chunar. This includes identifying and documenting archaeological sites and raising awareness about preserving the past.

With this background, the team inspected the area of the Chunar and documented the megalithic burials, rock paintings, microliths in detail.

Methodology of the work

1. Megalithic Burials

A detailed survey was conducted to identify the megalithic sites of the Chunar. A systematic documentation was conducted on the cemetery site to get minute details. Megaliths of each site were plotted, counted, numbered, and documented to see geo-coordinates, size, type, actual conditions, and elevation information. Each megalith was examined separately, with detailed documentation. Varies of types of equipment like GPS, Desto meter, and theodolite were used to get detailed information about the site. A systematic data sheet has been prepared to identify each megalith numerically, and the micro assessment of the individual megalith is recognised. The position of megaliths, the distance between each other, the present condition and the deposit have been documented. Each megalith has been numbered separately, divided into clusters and photographed to get maximum information. This documentation is helpful since tremendous human activity is responsible for the wipe-out of hundreds of megaliths on the site.

2. Microliths Collection

Explore the earlier reported microlithic sites to confirm their location. Dantari is marked as a type site, and systematic collection and documentation of microlithic tools are conducted here. To ensure accuracy and precision, a 10x10 meter grid was laid out, further divided into 1 square meter blocks, resulting in 100 blocks within the layout. Each block was meticulously examined and documented, following a consistent process. The microlithic tools were plotted within the 1x1 meter squares, enabling a detailed analysis of their spatial distribution. Comprehensive photographs were taken from various angles and corners, capturing the site's overall layout. The grid is located on the map as a trench layout. Additionally, close-up pictures of each block, both with and without scale and direction marks, were taken to provide accurate measurements and orientation. Hand drawings were prepared to supplement the visual documentation, offering an additional site representation. The undulated land formation of the layout was carefully studied, enhancing the understanding of the site's geological context. The collection focused on selected microlithic tools, encompassing finished products, unfinished items, fragments, and cores made from different semi-precious stone materials. Each artefact was collected only after meticulous documentation within its corresponding 1x1 meter block. This method ensures a comprehensive and detailed record of the systematic sampling, facilitating further analysis and interpretation of the microlithic tools from the Dantari Hill of Mirzapur.

3. Rock Art

Explore the earlier reported rock art sites of Chunar and trace out their conditions. For the micro-documentation of the painted rock shelter, detailed measurements were conducted at Dantari Hill. Based on the visible sandstone layers, the shelter was divided into five panels. Each panel, cluster, and individual painting was meticulously measured and photographed. D-Stretch is image enhancement software developed by Dr. John Harman used for rock art research. It utilises advanced algorithms to analyse digital images and enhance faded or invisible pictographs. By isolating and intensifying specific colour bands, the software enables the detection of faint pigments and intricate patterns that are otherwise indistinguishable from the naked eye. The D-Stretch software allowed us to identify intricate motifs, faded outlines, and superimpositions of earlier artworks that revealed layers of cultural activity over time. At Dantari rock shelters, we meticulously employed D-Stretch to uncover invisible pictographs under natural lighting conditions.

4. Habitation Sites

A systematic survey was conducted to understand the cultural deposit of habitation sites. The survey included micro-documentation, and the transverse method was employed. During the transverse process, the team gathered material remains from various parts of the mound. The centre of the mound was considered a midpoint, and pottery and related materials were collected from fixed distances in all directions. This technique allows an accurate estimation of the circumference and dimensions of the mound, the distribution of material remains within the mound, and the probable cultural deposit without excavation.

Scope of Work

The present work is unique in that megalithic burials, microliths, and rock art have been discovered and thoroughly documented. A survey confirmed the archaeological potential in the Chunar area, highlighting the need for extensive research. The megalithic burial sites are situated in the rock quarrying area of Chunar, where constant rock excavations have been carried out for a long. Due to the quarrying, several megaliths have been disturbed completely, and a whole landscape has been altered. Moreover, natives believe these megaliths are treasure spots, and many megaliths have been dug out and disturbed. Preserving this heritage is the primary concern of the study. This study was proposed and conducted since no detailed documentation work has ever been conducted in the Vindhyan megalithic complex. Similarly, the rock paintings of this area are exposed to human interventions and natural conditions. Documentation of rock paintings was also necessary before the paintings faded away. The rock shelters are also unprotected and threatened to be defaced by the art and graffiti of modern humans. Thus, micro-documentation was executed to get the minute details of each painting depicted on the rock shelter. The scope of this work is to save the prestigious heritage and prepare detailed documentation of the site for future purposes.

Discussion

The present survey and detailed investigation of megalithic burials, rock art, and microlith studies provide first-hand information about the various facets of the prehistoric and protohistoric cultural assets of Chunar. The first comprehensive documentation of megalithic burials and microliths is being conducted, which provides valuable insights into several aspects of their culture. This survey was fruitful for understanding the lives of first settlers, beliefs, and customs and contributing to a deeper understanding of our heritage.

Chapter 2
The Area

Virag G. Sontakke and Sachin Kr. Tiwary

Mirzapur, located in south-eastern Uttar Pradesh, is a region of significant geographical importance. The district lies in the Vindhyachal region, surrounded by Bhadohi and Varanasi from the north, Chandauli on the east, Sonbhadra from the south, and Prayagraj from the northwest. Two physiographic units divide the district, namely the northern alluvial tract and the southern hilly area. Forming part of the Gangetic plain, the northern alluvial tract is a flat land with a regional slope towards the north. In contrast, the Southern Hills Area is a tableland that rises abruptly from the northern alluvial tract with an escarpment, forming the northern fringe of the Vindhyan plateau. The Southern part falls within the geological domain of the Vindhyan Supergroup, characterised by a diverse stratigraphic profile contributing to its distinctive geographical landscape. The geological composition primarily consists of stratified layers, prominently featuring the Kaimur formation, the Rewa Hill range, older and newer alluvium deposits, and significant occurrences of ferruginous gravels (Bhukosh 2024). Ancient human beings have utilised these diverse geophysical conditions since the prehistoric period. The present research mainly focuses on Dantari Hill, wherein varied cultural materials have been identified.

Chunar

Chunar is a place of profound historical significance steeped in a rich millennia history. Small hills grace the southern part of Chunar, while the Ganga River embraces the northern side, offering a vast plain that has fostered diverse human activities over the ages. Geographically, Chunar is nestled in the northeastern part of the Vindhya range, and administratively, it is situated in the eastern part of the Mirzapur district. Its rich and diverse cultural heritage is evidenced by the myriad of archaeological remains scattered throughout the region, providing invaluable insights into the ancient past. The prehistoric period in Chunar is marked by an abundance of stone tools and artefacts, indicating the presence of early human settlements (Tewari 1997: 51-58; 1999: 163-223; Kumar 2022). In proto-historic times, abundant evidence of megalithic cemeteries has been encountered in the hilly regions of southern Chunar (Mesurier 1867: 164-166;

Carlleyle 1883: 49-55; Cunningham 1871; Tewari 1997: 51-58; 1999: 163-223; Kumar 2022). Painted rock shelters located at hills contain depictions of hunting scenes, war scenes, and ritualistic activities (Tewari 1997: 51-58; 1999: 163-223; Kumar 2022). This region is also rich in early historical evidence. There is evidence that stones were quarried from these areas for constructing Ashoka's Pillar during the Maurya period (Pant and Jayaswal 1990: 49-52). Stone carving activities persisted even after Ashoka's time, as confirmed by structures found in the surrounding areas (Kaur et al 2019: 1771-1783). Stone quarrying is still active in these regions today. This evidence highlights the archaeological significance of Chunar, proving that the area has been a hub of human activity since ancient times.

Dantari Hill

Dantari is a small hilly area located in the southern hilly tract of Chunar tehsil in the Mirzapur district of Uttar Pradesh (Fig. 2.1). The Hill is approximately 50 km east of the Mirzapur district headquarters, 15 km south of Chunar, and 45 km south of Varanasi. Geographically, the Hill is situated in the Kaimur Hill range, part of the Vindhyan mountains, and positioned south of the Ganga River. At present, Jargo, one of the largest dams in the Mirzapur district, is located adjacent to a hill that restricts its eastern extent. Additionally, the areas of Dhaunha, Baheri, Bahera, Banimilia, and Kumhia encircle Dantari Hill. Dantari Hill is regarded as a religious place by the locals. According to local belief, a hidden golden temple lies within the hill, overseen by the deity *'Dantabir Baba'*, from whom the hill derives its name. Additionally, there is another explanation for its name. The hill is abundant with microliths made of chert, chalcedony, and agate, which the locals refer to as *"Budhiya ke Daant"* (teeth of an old woman). Thus, the hill is known as Dantari due to these tooth-like stones.

Environment Settings

Mirzapur has distinct geographical features characterised by small hills and plains. As stated earlier, the southeastern part of the district is rich with small barren hills, while to the north, flat fertile plains formed by the Ganga River. Geographically, this area falls within the northeastern periphery of the Vindhya Range, marked by a diverse stratigraphic profile (Fig. 2.2). The Kaimur formation, dating back to the Mesoproterozoic era, makes up a significant portion of the

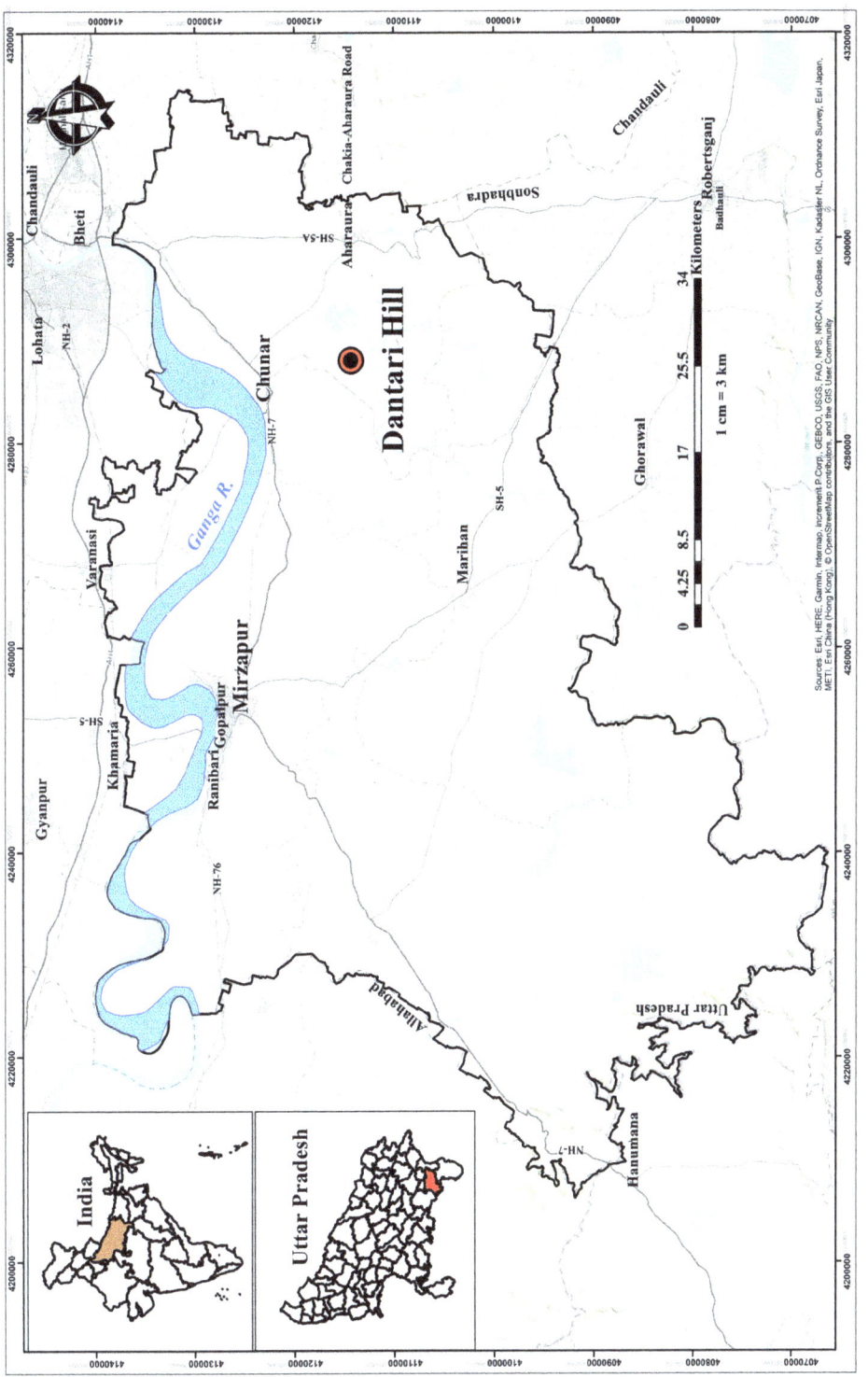

Fig. 2.1. Location map of Dantari Hill, Mirzapur District, Uttar Pradesh

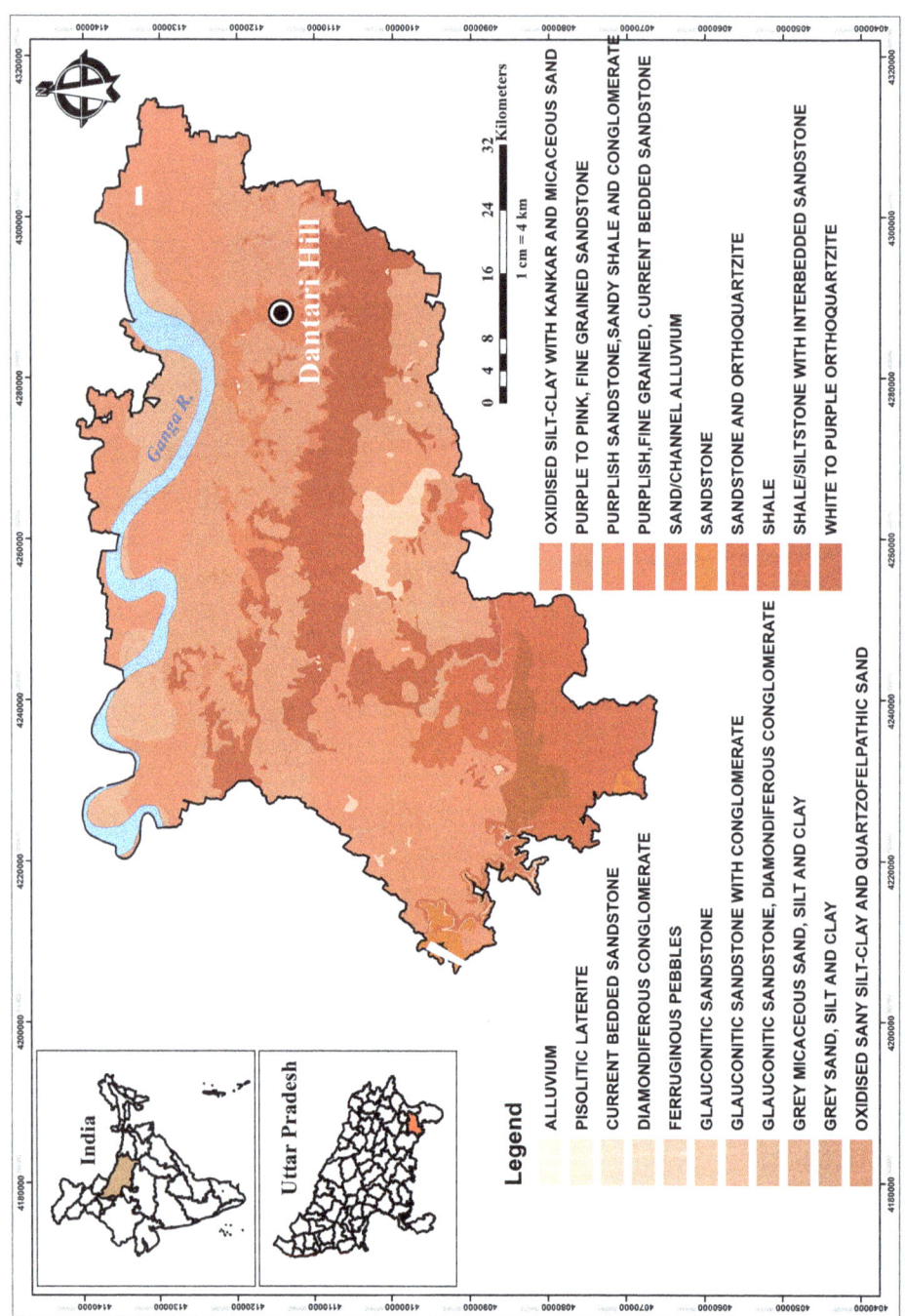

Fig. 2.2. Lithology map of Mirzapur District, Uttar Pradesh

sedimentary layers (Bhukosh 2024). The older alluvium, which dates to the early-middle Pleistocene age, is a prominent component of the geological landscape of Chunar. Several major rock types, including sandstone, quartzofeldspathic, conglomerate, and orthoquartzite, characterise Chunar geology. Other significant lithological formations in the district include shale, grey sand, micaceous sand, ferruginous pebbles, and pisolitic laterite. Sandstone occurs notably in bedded formations, displaying distinct hues of purple and pink (Bhukosh 2024). The archaeological site of Dantari Hill is nestled within these purple sandstone formations.

The Chunar area features varied elevations. On the flat plains of northern Chunar, the elevation ranges from 31 to 100 meters above sea level, making it the lowest point in the district. Small hills emerge from north to south, with elevations ranging from 100 to 150 meters, including Dantari Hill (Fig. 2.3). Further south, the altitude gradually increases and reaches its peak in the western part. On the Rewa Hill range, the highest elevation is approximately 450 meters. Along the northern boundary of the district, the Ganga River flows, creating fertile plains and traversing several rivers. Other significant rivers include the Belan, Pachbahani, Adwa, Odda, and Karmanasha. These rivers and numerous smaller streams contribute to the region's agricultural viability and support diverse ecosystems.

The fertile plains in the northern part of Chunar, enriched by the Ganga River, support a variety of crops. Major crops include paddy, wheat, barley, and pulses cultivated during the Kharif and Rabi seasons (Brockman 1911: 50-51). Sugarcane and vegetables are also grown extensively, benefiting from the region's favourable climatic conditions and irrigation facilities. In the southern hilly areas, terraced farming is practised to grow crops such as millets, pulses, and oilseeds. The district's diverse topography and soil types enable a wide range of agricultural activities. A network of rivers provides perennial water sources to support irrigation, further enhancing agricultural productivity and sustainability in Chunar. Recent data from the Center for Hydrometeorology and Remote Sensing (CHRS) indicate that the district's average annual rainfall ranged from 1502 to 1863 mm (Average rainfall data 2024). This significant increase in rainfall has implications for the district's agriculture, water resources, and overall climate patterns, causing updated water management and agricultural planning strategies to adapt to these changing conditions (Fig. 2.4).

The area is home to diverse flora and wildlife, representing its diverse ecosystems. The region's flora combines tropical and subtropical

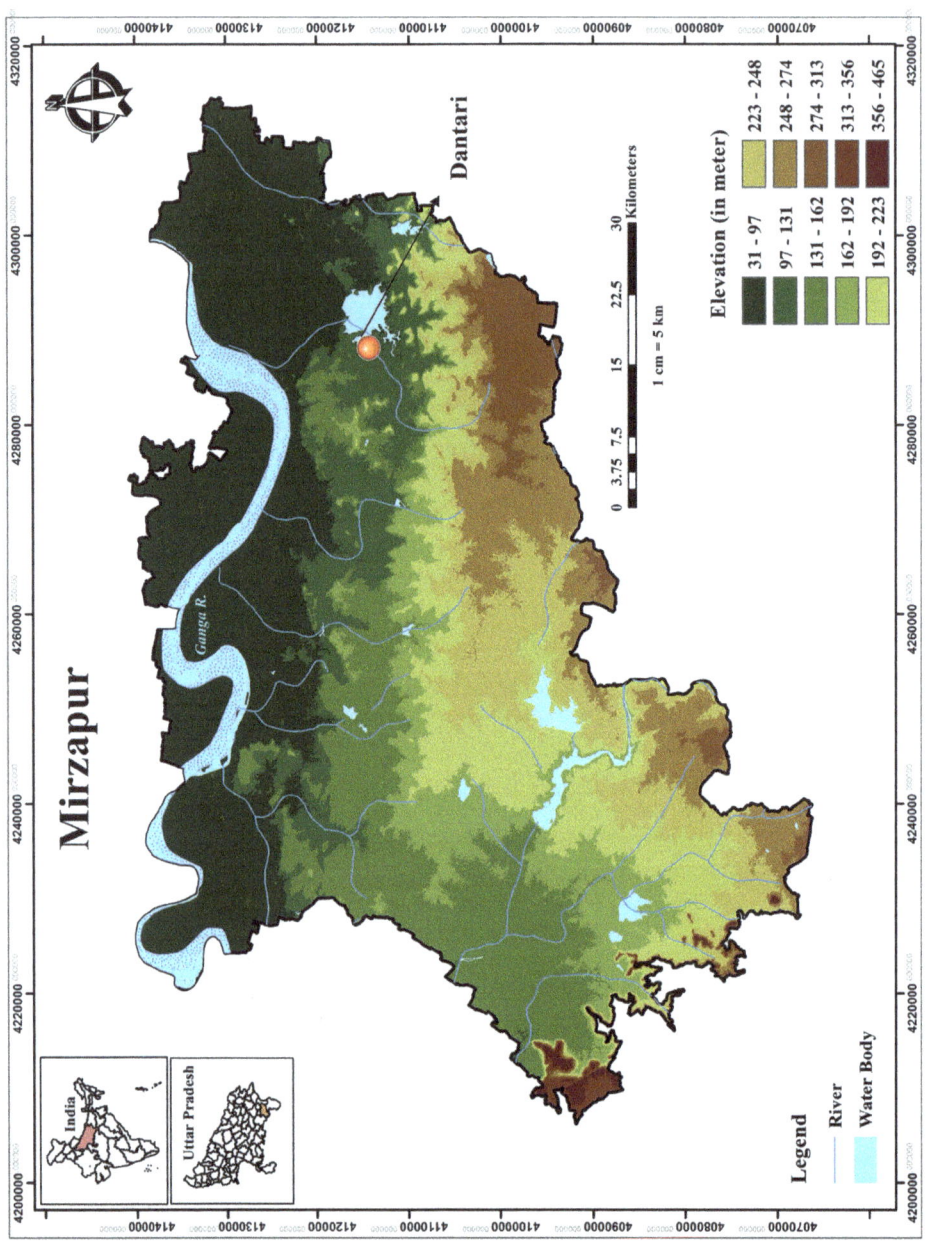

Fig. 2.3. Elevation map of Mirzapur District, Uttar Pradesh

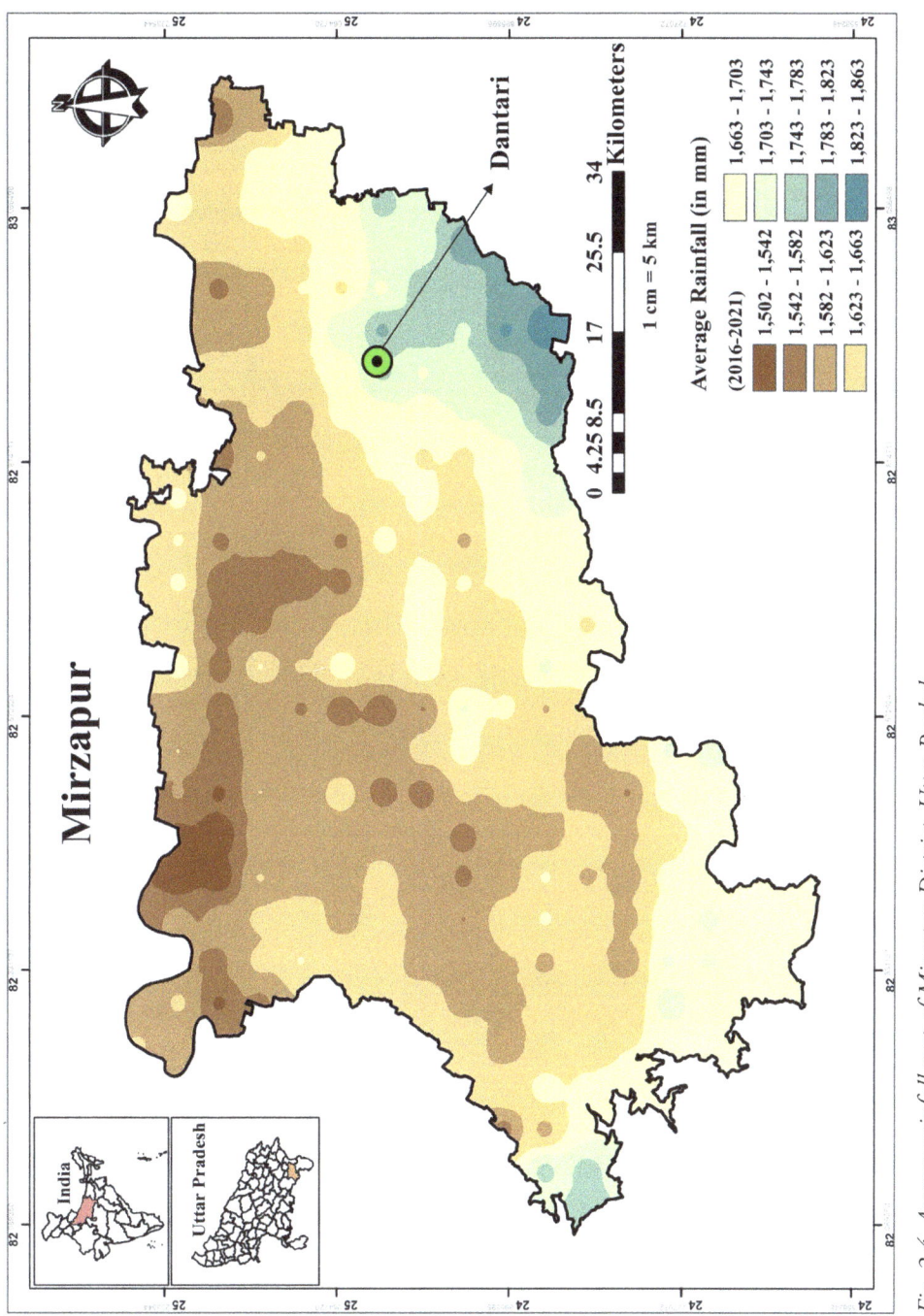

Fig. 2.4. Average rainfall map of Mirzapur District, Uttar Pradesh

vegetation with dense woods, grasslands, and riverine habitats. Common tree species include *teak, sal, mahua*, and several medicinal herbs (Brockman 1911: 37). Wildlife in Mirzapur includes deer, wild boar, monkeys, and a variety of bird species, which contribute to the district's biodiversity.

Chunar is noted for its mineral reserves, which include sandstone, quartzite, limestone, and coal (Brockman 1911: 22; Kaur et *al.* 2019: 1771-1783). These resources have historically supported regional industries and economic activities, but sustainable management approaches are becoming increasingly important in balancing conservation and development goals. The region is home to diverse indigenous tribal communities, such as the Kharwar, Gond, Kol, Baiga, and Agariya tribes. These groups have distinct cultural traditions, dialects, and subsistence methods firmly based on the region's natural resources. Agriculture, handicrafts, and forestry are traditional professions, and certain tribes are well-known for their expertise in specific crafts.

Discussion

This diverges geophysical features, ecological niches, and suitable environments, which played a vital role in shaping the human adaptation of Mirzapur. Abundant flora, fauna, plenty of water resources, and a natural landscape could have attracted man to settle in the region. Several rock paintings and hunting scenes aptly present the region's ancient scenario. Mineral resources and the availability of the rocky surface probably were one of the primary reasons that the megalithic communities were attracted to the area.

Chapter 3
Megaliths of Dantari Hill: Typology, Placement and Locational Analysis

Virag G. Sontakke and Dheeraj Sharma

Burying the dead is one of the oldest customs of human beings. The Neanderthals buried their dead approximately 130,000 years ago, which reflects their developing psyche and emotional quotient. The practice of burying the deceased in India traces its origins to the Mesolithic period, particularly in the Ganga plain. At the onset of the Holocene period, the area experienced substantial changes due to increased population, primarily due to heightened rainfall and its influence on the local flora and fauna. These chain reactions may have led to the first colonisation of the Ganga period. Megalithic culture is always the most vital period for understanding the significance and nuances of the burial system. Primarily, it was considered that the Megalithic period coincided with the Iron Age in India. Many megalithic burials were discovered in Mirzapur, one of the significant nuclei in Uttar Pradesh.

Megalith refers to constructing massive stone structures, typically associated with burial sites or assembled from large collected stones. The term originates from Greek roots: *'megas,'* meaning large, and *'lithos,'* meaning stone. Essentially, 'megalith' describes the monumental stone structures built atop burial sites. The term was first introduced in 1849 by Algernon Herbert to explain the archaeological site of Stonehenge in Britain (Herbert 1849). Megalithic tombs exist in various parts of the world and have unique names specific to their respective locations. For example, people in France and Spain refer to them as 'dolmens', while in Portugal, they are called 'antas'. Cromlechs are their name in Wales, whereas in England and Scotland, they are known as 'cairns' and 'barrows'. They are called 'dysser' in Denmark, and in Sardinia, they are known as 'tombe di giganti'. In India, native names like '*bhiraharis*', '*kodey kulls*', '*topie kulls*', '*kuda*', '*dhuha*', and others are used. The practice of constructing megaliths for burials is witnessed not only in India but also has parallels in different parts of the world. In India, megaliths are considered burial structures made of stones that were constructed during the early Iron Age and the Early Historical period. However, Urn-burial, which avoids the use of stones, is also known as a megalith due to its cultural similarities.

Megaliths exist in multiple parts of India, but in South India they are heavily concentrated. States like Tamilnadu, Kerala, Karnataka and Andhra Pradesh bear the maximum number of megalithic sites, followed by Telangana and Vidarbha. This area has also been the focus of most studies on megalithic burials. This region has remained an area of attraction for archaeologists for a long time. Only the reporting of the megaliths and a few excavations in the Vindhyan area could not tell us the precise identity of this culture in this specific region. Since this was a serious issue, a team explored the area to get a clear understanding of the megaliths of the region. During their explorations, the team came across several megalithic burial sites, along with Dantari Hill. The vast concentration of megaliths at the Dantari, its location, and the nature of the megaliths were taken into consideration for the detailed investigations.

Dantari Hill is situated in the Chunar block of the Mirzapur district. The nearest village from the Dantari Hill is Baheri. On Dantari Hill, the megalithic cemetery site occupies most of the area, excluding the east. East to west, the cemetery site spans approximately 2.60 km, while north to south it measures approximately 1.70 km. The megaliths are situated all along the hill at different elevations. Several perennial water sources, including the Pachbahani River (south), Vishva Shanti Dari (west), and Pakadi Nala (north), surround the hill. Dantari Hill is the largest megalithic cemetery site in the Vindhya region so far, constituting about 500 megaliths. Hitherto, such a concentration of megaliths has not been reported on any site.

Methodology Adopted

The following methodology was adopted for this study to document and analyse the identified burial sites comprehensively.

1. **Micro-documentation of megaliths:** To understand the megaliths of the area, micro-documentation of megalithic burials was undertaken. This documentation included recording the geo-coordinates, diameter, type, current deposit, directional orientation, and overall characteristics of each megalith. To facilitate accurate data collection, various tools and equipment, such as GPS, Destometer, and theodolite, were utilised. This allowed for precise measurements and detailed information gathering about the site (Fig. 3.1).
2. **Cluster Classification:** Each megalith is assigned a unique number for identification. We divided the cemetery into five

Fig. 3.1. Micro-documentation of megalithic burial at Dantari Hill

clusters, A to E, taking into consideration the geophysical conditions of the area and the placement of the megaliths. We also considered the type of megalith, its location, elevation, and position for documentation purposes.

3. **Surface Collection:** Material remains from the surface of megaliths and their surrounding areas were collected systematically. This involved a collection of pottery, tools, and other objects associated with the megaliths.
4. **Photography:** Comprehensive photography of each megalith was conducted from various angles to ensure thorough documentation. This visual record was aimed at facilitating future studies and analyses, even in the event of destruction or alteration of the burial sites.

Typology of Megaliths

Cairns are the most widespread type of megaliths found in Chunar, showing a consistent typology. Several scholars' earlier explorations of the region also highlighted the cairns as a chief type. On Dantari Hill, two main types of megaliths have been popular: cairns, which are the most abundant, and cists within cairns. However, during the current survey, a new type of megalithic burial, menhir within cairn, has also been discovered (Fig. 3.2).

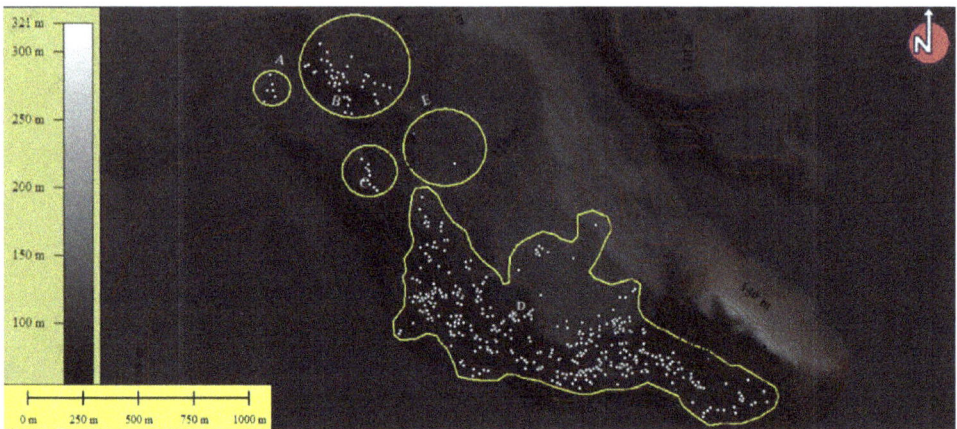

Fig. 3.2. Distribution of megalithic burials at Dantari Hil

a) Cairn:

Cairns are typically made of loose, unworked stones of varying sizes and are often marked by small mounds. Due to their accessibility, sandstone blocks were commonly used in the composition of cairns. The diameters of these cairns range from 2 to 20 meters, containing various types of deposits. Previous excavations in Mirzapur have provided insight into the construction techniques of these megaliths. Cairns were built by digging a pit into the natural soil. If grave goods were present, they were placed at the bottom, followed by a layer of excavated soil and loose stones. The arrangement of burial goods varied, with a concentration of stones often found at the top, especially if a cist was absent. So far, no reports have mentioned individual cists in the Chunar area (Fig. 3.3).

b) Cist within cairns:

This is the second most common type after cairns. To construct a cist, a pit was dug into the natural soil, and cist slabs were erected, with soil and stone blocks packed on either side to secure the orthostats. If grave goods were present, they were placed at the bottom before the cairn was filled with excavated material. Unlike those found in South India, the cists in Chunar are made of multiple small stones stacked to create vertical walls for a box-like chamber topped with visible capstones. These cists are small, lack portholes, and are mostly in an early stage of development, although some single-stone orthostats were also utilised. Positioned at the centre of a cairn, the cists are covered by loose stones forming a heap (Fig. 3.4).

Megaliths of Dantari Hill: Typology, Placement and Locational Analysis

Fig. 3.3. Cairn type of megalith at Dantari Hill

Fig. 3.4. Cist within cairn type of megalith at Dantari Hill

c) Menhir within cairn:

For the first time, menhir within cairns is a new type reported in the Vindhya. In this, a vertical stone was erected at the centre of the cairn and capped by a loose stone deposit. Each menhir within the cairns has been broken from the top. It is believed that the natives reused the menhir stone slab for household activity (Fig. 3.5).

d) Menhir

This is again a new type found in the Chunar area. Recent exploration revealed a few independent menhirs in the cemetery. These menhirs are usually one to two meters high, and most have a deliberate triangular shape at the top. Though, their numbers are limited as compared to other types.

Distribution of megaliths at Dantari Hill

The megaliths spread across different locations and elevations around the hill. Based on the arrangement of the megaliths, their typology, the existence of rain channels, height, and location of the area, they are divided into five clusters: A, B, C, D, and E. Cluster-A was located in the western part of the hill. Cluster B, positioned northeast of Cluster-A,

Fig. 3.5. Menhir within cairn type of megalith at Dantari Hill

was separated by *Siddha Shanti Dari*. South of this, a distinct group of megaliths formed Cluster- C. The largest group, Cluster- D, covered the entire southern area of the hill, documenting maximum megaliths of different types. Two individual megaliths in an isolated area belonged to Cluster-E. Each cluster has unique characteristics, such as landscape, rain gullies, slopes, separate types, and proximity to neighbouring megaliths. The spaces between the clusters are geographically and typologically distinct. These empty spaces likely reflect social practices, beliefs, customs of the deceased, and possibly ancestral affiliations.

Quantitative Enquiry of Megaliths

A survey on Dantari Hill revealed nearly five hundred megalithic burials spread across different locations and elevations. These megaliths were predominantly on the surface, with some natural elements like rain rivulets, flatlands, and rugged terrain dividing them. Among the documented megaliths, the cairn type is the most popular, totalling 420. Cist within cairns are the second most common megalithic type after cairns numbering 56. The third category includes menhir within cairns, with six specimens in the area. At this site, cists and menhirs are found only inside the cairns; however, a subsequent exploration revealed a few independent menhirs in the cemetery (Fig. 3.6).

After classifying the clusters, each megalith of the separate cluster was documented typologically. Cairn types of megaliths were found in all the clusters, followed by the cist within cairn. However, the latter type is significantly less restricted only in clusters B and C. Similarly, menhir within cairns appear in limited numbers and are only present in Cluster D. The type-wise distribution of the Dantari megaliths testifies the cairn was a principal type (Fig. 3.7).

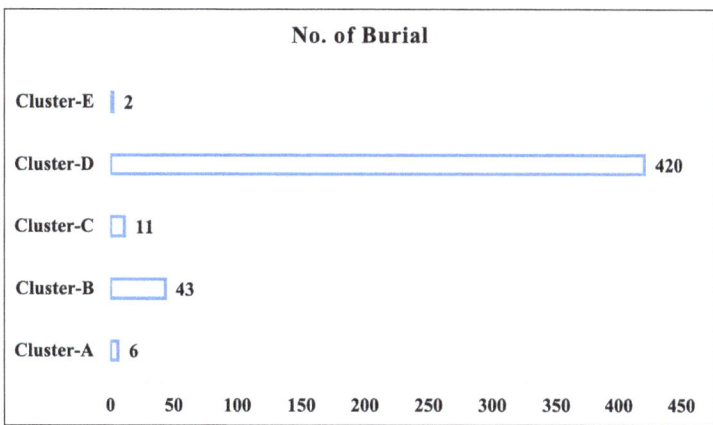

Fig. 3.6. Cluster-wise distributions of the megaliths at Dantari Hill

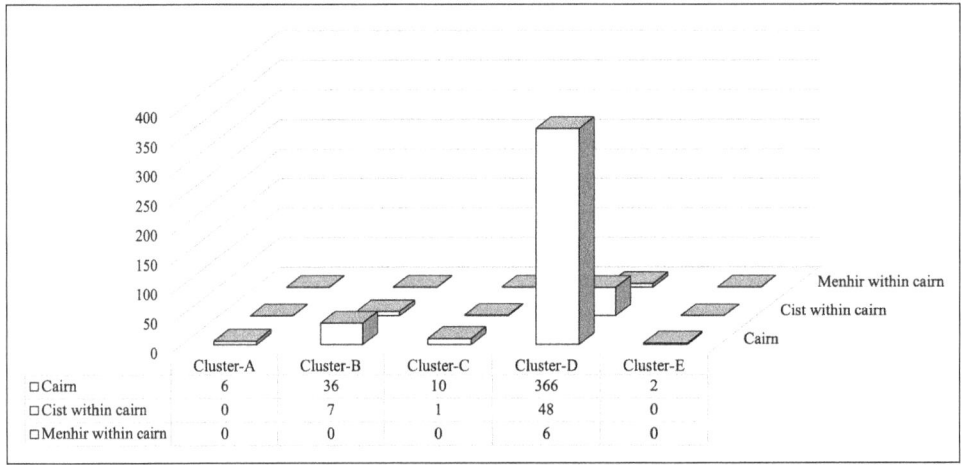

Fig. 3.7. Type-wise distributions of the megaliths at Dantari Hill

Locational Analysis of the Megaliths

The megaliths are spread across different hill slopes in the Dantari Hill, indicating the most preferred area. After the micro-documentation process, it was found that there were 14 megaliths on the eastern side of the hill, 40 on the western side, six on the northern side, 376 on the southern side, and 46 in the centre of the hill. The available data shows that people favoured constructing burials on the southern slope. The Pachbahani River flows along the south slope of Dantari Hill, which is likely why this area was chosen for burial construction (Fig. 3.8).

During documentation of the megalithic cemetery area, different sizes of megaliths were found and recorded. Each megalith underwent a thorough assessment and classification based on its size, with distinctions made between large (over 10 meters), medium (5-10 meters), and small (1-5 meters) sizes. The prevalence of medium-

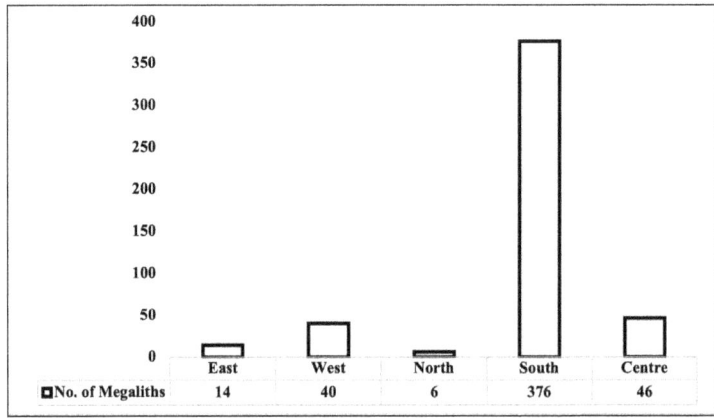

Fig. 3.8. The placement of megaliths in different areas of the Dantari Hill

sized megaliths was notable, with the largest megaliths falling within this category (Fig. 3.9).

The megaliths have been reported from different locations on the Dantari Hill. The minute plotting of megaliths located at varying elevations of hills brought exciting outcomes. Only 46 megaliths were found at the base of the hill. The 110-125 meters from the Main Sea Level seemed preferable for megalith constructions. This area contains the majority of megaliths erected close to one another. It was also observed that the flat surface at the top of the hill served as a burial ground, albeit with relatively fewer megaliths than the mid elevation zone (Fig. 3.10).

Megaliths and Human Destruction

Apart from other archaeological findings, megaliths are unique because of their distinct structure. Unlike other archaeological

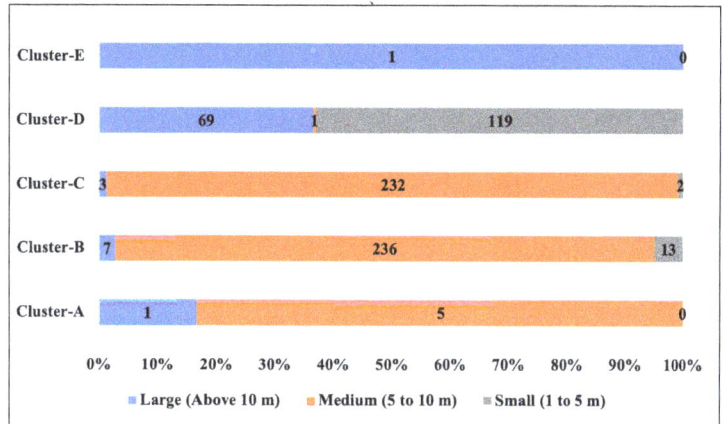

Fig. 3.9. Size-wise distributions of the megaliths at Dantari Hill

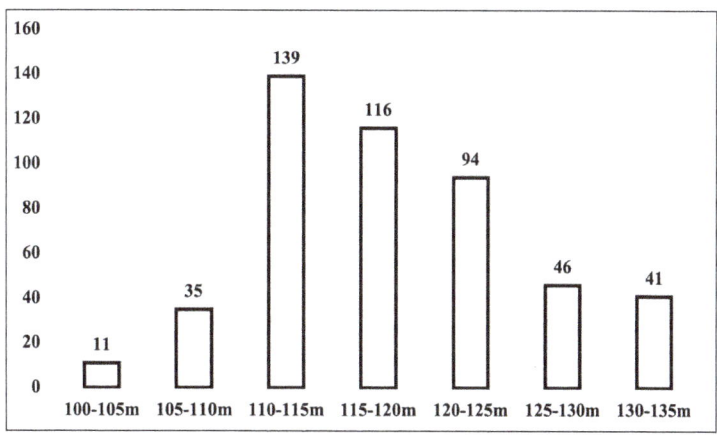

Fig. 3.10. Distribution of the megaliths according to the elevation of Dantari Hill

vestiges, megaliths are usually found on top of the ground and can be easily identified from their distinct structure, even by the commoners. There were many cists within cairn on the site, and these were seen to be dug out from the centre. Locally, these megaliths are referred to as '*Bhirihari*'. A popular belief surrounds these megaliths, suggesting that the Banjara people buried their wealth in these megaliths and enchanted them with witchcraft. According to this legend, if the '*Bhirihari*' are excavated, the treasure within turns to ashes because of the magical spells. Locals dug up and disturbed plenty of megaliths to extract the treasure beneath (Fig. 3.11). Megalithic burials with high deposits are often found dug in the centre. Even Le Mesurier, in 1867, discovered many such megaliths, which the natives destroyed to get the supposed wealth.

Geologically, the area of Chunar is rich because of the availability of many rich resources. It is evident from historical sources that Mauryan King Ashoka utilised the sandstones of this area to create pillars and architectural structures. Thus, several rock quarrying operations have been conducted to extract the Chunar sandstones from this area. The Chunar sandstones remained popular sources for architecture and art throughout Indian history. Even today, these rocks continue to be utilised for civil work, such as building houses, roads, drains, canals, and construction of dams. In the present times, it is evident that several megalithic cemetery sites are destroyed due to rock quarries in and around Chunar.

Fig. 3.11. Vandalised megalith at Dantari Hill

Fig. 3.12: Destruction of megalith showing the construction pattern

This current study also measures the destruction of megaliths caused by human and natural destruction. Numerous megaliths in the area have been partially or almost disturbed (Fig. 3.12). The disturbances allow us to classify the megaliths into three divisions like almost disturbed, partially disturbed and intact. Those megaliths dug up, excavated, or quarried and represented only by a few stones are categorised as almost disturbed. Megaliths that are partially dug or have their stones removed are documented under the partially disturbed category. Those that seem undisturbed, complete and in the original manifestation are categorised as intact (Fig. 3.13).

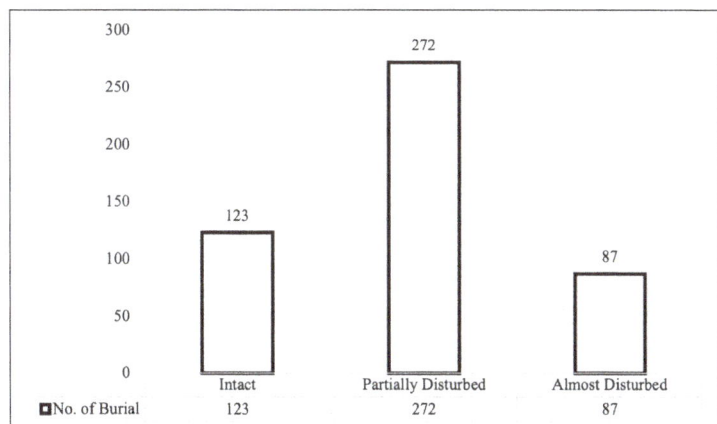

Fig. 3.13. The present quantity of the megaliths according to their conditions

The Construction Pattern of Megaliths

As stated above, natives have dug several megaliths at the centre to extract treasure. These disturbed megaliths provide a valuable source for understanding the construction pattern of the megaliths. A popular megalithic type cairn was generally erected directly upon the surface using stones and soil interchangeably, raising the height. A circular structure was formed by organising loose rocks. Stones ranging from approximately 10 to 80 cm have been used to raise the deposit at the centre. It was also noticed that the base of the megalith has more soil, while the quantity of stone progressively increases towards the top. For the cist within the cairn, the central pit was dug. Usually, capstones are visible at the top of the cairn deposit. Menhir within the cairn also follows a similar pattern where vertical slabs are erected in the base.

Artefacts and Key Features

Several items were found on the surface and inside the disturbed megaliths during the documentation of megalithic burials. Usually, broken potsherds were found inside the disturbed megaliths. Plenty of microliths are also found in various localities of Dantari Hill. All

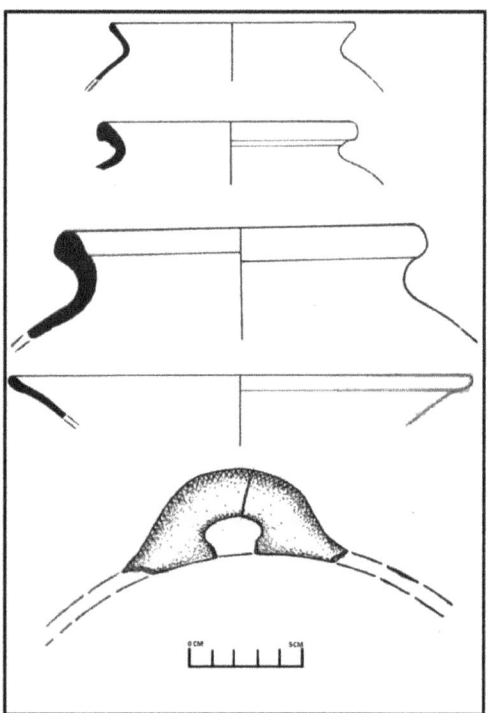

Fig. 3.14. Ceramics recovered from megalithic burials at Dantari Hill

these objects were systematically collected and documented. Their description is given below.

Pottery

Pottery is one of the primary sources from which characteristics about the past can be understood. Usually, pottery is the most abundant find in archaeological sites. However, pottery is a rare find in the case of megaliths. The potsherds collected from Dantari megaliths are ordinary and ill-fired mainly consist of coarse red ware comprising small bowls, pots, and miniature vases. Most of the potsherds found from the site show signs of wear, which could point to its age of deposition, which was not in the near past. There were also a few sherds with red slip coating. The pottery unearthed from the surface at Dantari Hill resembles those found in the megaliths of Banimilia Bahera (IAR 1962-63: 38-39). The surface treatment, shapes, and firing techniques indicate that this pottery was likely crafted specifically for megalithic burials possibly for ceremonial offerings (Fig. 3.14).

Microliths

The presence of microliths in megalithic burials is a unique characteristic of the Vindhyan megaliths. Microliths are an identifying feature of the Mesolithic, Neolithic and Chalcolithic periods. Previous excavations

Fig. 3.15. Stone disks recovered from the top of megalithic burials

at Banimilia Bahera revealed numerous microliths and waste chips within the megalithic burials (IAR 1962-63:38-39). A similar burial custom, placing microliths in graves, was also shown in the megaliths of Adwa Valley. The megaliths of Kakoria, Magha, and Tokwa yielded many microliths made from chert, chalcedony, and agate. Burials in the Adwa Valley contained microliths of chert, chalcedony, and agate, reflecting a shared practice (Misra et.*al.* 2014: 342-375). Numerous microliths were also gathered inside and around the megaliths on Dantari Hill, displaying similarities with those from Adwa Valley.

Stone Disks

While surveying the megaliths of Dantari Hill, several circular stone disks have been reported. These circular stone disks made of sandstone, are placed at the top of the megalithic burials. Their placement and fine workmanship indicate the customary behaviour of the megaliths of Dantari. These stone disks are varied in size, ranging from a minimum diameter of 2.5 cm to a maximum of 10 cm (Fig. 3.15). No earlier excavated sites of the Mirzapur reported such stone disks. A similar kind of stone disk is also observed in the megaliths of Adwa Valley. This shows the stone disks are the typical mark of the megaliths of the Vindhyan region. The overall nature, manufacturing process, and placement of the stone disks over the megaliths suggest that people probably used them as offerings in mortuary practice.

Discussion

The above overview of the megalithic sites of the Dantari Hill and adjoining area suggests this area was one of the most suitable for a megalithic cemetery. Megalithic burial sites are located on rocky outcrops and have similar architecture. The cairn is popular, followed by cist within the cairn and menhir within the cairn. The geophysical settings played a vital role in shaping the megaliths in the region. Loose stones were used frequently in the erection of cist and cairns, whereas complete rocks were used in the capstones. Size, deposit, and placement of megaliths reflect the socio-political hierarchy. The big sizes of megaliths, like cist within cairns and cairns, are a few compared to the medium-sized cairns, hint the same. The number of megaliths differs from site to site, yet some locations produced a massive quantity, suggesting a favoured area. Dantari Hill is the only cemetery in the area which retains nearly 500 megalithic burials in one place. The vast number of megaliths in one place also indicates the significance of Dantari in ritual and mortuary customs.

Table 3.1. List of megalithic sites of the Mirzapur district, Uttar Pradesh

Sr. No.	Site	Latitude	Longitude	Nature
1	Pokhara	24.62614538	82.35670961	Habitation & Burial
2	Karaundaha	24.68356725	82.33336548	Burial
3	Kawaljhar	24.71277288	82.32216855	Habitation & Burial
4	Songarha	24.73356715	82.29997854	Habitation & Burial
5	Cherulahwa Dandi	24.40025402	82.31663451	Burial
6	Patharahia Dandi	24.76688101	82.3167418	Burial
7	Baidha	24.77880591	82.31829038	Burial
8	Kothi Khurd	24.25716448	82.31864691	Burial
9	Kothi Kalan	24.78487803	82.31806633	Burial
10	Tikuri (Ahugi Kalan)	24.62606736	82.31824747	Burial
11	Madhor	24.79474632	82.32490344	Habitation & Burial
12	Hathera	24.81131559	82.33841913	Burial
13	Pura Awasan Singh	24.827992	82.3033333	Burial
14	Kotar	24.84195877	82.30440148	Habitation & Burial
15	Sarahara	24.8480017	82.28324747	Burial
16	Pathera	24.86465854	82.2666667	Burial
17	Bedaur	24.86685163	82.28336548	Burial
18	Chitaha	24.87740712	82.29163451	Burial
19	Khuntabir	24.8853017	82.27275634	Burial
20	Naugawan	24.89967794	82.27283144	Burial
21	Tokwa	24.90023354	82.28326892	Habitation & Burial
22	Magha	24.61692028	82.31237125	Habitation & Burial
23	Adhesar Hill	24.62527307	82.30660232	Burial
24	Jhaprahwa	24.60439104	82.3068169	Burial
25	Parsia	24.61133543	82.36158087	Habitation & Burial
26	Gaurwa	24.61126715	82.36258583	Habitation & Burial
27	Karaundahia	24.61466872	82.39327965	Habitation & Burial
28	Indari	24.62741724	82.3332582	Habitation & Burial

Sr. No.	Site	Latitude	Longitude	Nature
29	Rampur	24.61182275	82.3683333	Habitation & Burial
30	Baraunha	24.64237821	82.34997854	Habitation & Burial
31	Banjari or Ganjaria	24.68348926	82.36447658	Habitation & Burial
32	Tita	24.68354775	82.36473293	Habitation & Burial
33	Deori	24.65941044	82.3477027	Burial
34	Chaura	24.66910338	82.3966667	Habitation & Burial
35	Laimanpur	24.67746591	82.35327965	Burial
36	Pipra	24.68073106	82.3211111	Habitation & Burial
37	Sukta	24.68552149	82.33837621	Habitation & Burial
38	Gurgi	24.75439077	82.33830111	Burial
39	Bahera	25.00815	82.89071	Habitation & Burial
40	Jaugarh	24.96371212	82.81502495	Burial
41	Sakteshgarh	24.98794061	82.76323959	Burial
42	Barji	25.27102	82.99472	Burial
43	Barakaccha	25.03781	82.74667	Burial
44	Chitampur	25.07953	82.60231	Burial
45	Lower Khajuri Dam	25.07953	82.60231	Burial
46	Karanpur Devpur	N.A.	N.A.	Burial
47	Arjunapur-Lauriya	N.A.	N.A.	Burial
48	Maina Pahar	25.01366	82.90532	Burial
49	Lakhimpur	N.A.	N.A.	Burial
50	Lalpurawa	N.A.	N.A.	Burial
51	Garbata-Raja	N.A.	N.A.	Burial
52	Pathraha	N.A.	N.A.	Burial
53	Banbaira Pahar (Nikarika)	N.A.	N.A.	Burial
54	Lekhania (North of Nikarika)	24.89667111	82.89	Burial
55	Lekhania (Near Rajapur)	24.92161267	82.71384598	Burial

Sr. No.	Site	Latitude	Longitude	Nature
56	Lusa	24.88600847	82.8011111	Burial
57	Raikari	24.8524461	82.7655556	Burial
58	Bandheta	N.A.	N.A.	Burial
59	Bari	24.89714875	82.2941667	Burial
60	Birpur	24.80436147	82.27940148	Burial
61	Chitarwar	24.97825009	82.33330111	Burial
62	Chaura	24.66991718	82.40829038	Burial
63	Chunawa	24.78964893	82.35811997	Burial
64	Devapur	N.A.	N.A.	Burial
65	Devari	N.A.	N.A.	Burial
66	Ghaghawa	N.A.	N.A.	Burial
67	Siddha Nath Ki Dari	24.96897	82.82218	Burial
68	Itar	24.75021434	82.30008583	Burial
69	Jaraha	24.98962915	82.41743562	Burial
70	Titwa Pahar	25.03175	82.84404	Burial
71	Kubara	24.79777269	82.35310924	Burial
72	Kulkamkalan	24.95803068	82.4577778	Burial
73	Kaluha	25.02602772	82.45786363	Burial
74	Bajahur	24.99825	82.89348	Burial
75	Siyanhara	25.04938	82.90897	Burial
76	Kumhia	25.031088	82.91288	Burial
77	Maheshpur Muraw	N.A.	N.A.	Burial
78	Naugawan	24.89966821	82.27271342	Burial
79	Rampur-38	25.01787	82.85879	Burial
80	Marihan	24.94884455	82.69473293	Burial
81	Gobardaha	24.90911269	83.00587621	Burial
82	Pokharaud	24.90558918	82.7947222	Burial
83	Bishunpur	24.91204589	82.77947183	Burial
84	Bhuluhia Pahari	24.95492646	82.67475438	Burial

Sr. No.	Site	Latitude	Longitude	Nature
85	Bhawanipur	24.89970714	82.67477584	Burial
86	Medharia	24.92127649	83.00431565	Burial
87	Kharian	25.04872	82.93434	Burial
88	Semari	24.91973628	82.8697973	Burial
89	Pokhraud	24.90318	82.81504	Burial
90	Magha- Manigara	N.A.	N.A.	Habitation & Burial
91	Pernia	N.A.	N.A.	Burial
92	Talaiya	24.90654	82.83356	Burial
93	Samudwa	25.01787	82.85879	Burial
94	Baghmania	N.A.	N.A.	Burial
95	Chhilahina	N.A.	N.A.	Habitation & Burial
96	Patita	N.A.	N.A.	Habitation & Burial
97	Aguhi-Kalan	N.A.	N.A.	Habitation & Burial
98	Manoharpur	25.03569	82.72679	Burial

Chapter 4
Microliths of Dantari Hill

Dheeraj Sharma, Sachin Kr. Tiwary and Pratik Pandey

Microlithic tools are small, typically measuring less than 5 cm, and are often crafted from crypto-crystalline silica-rich raw materials. These tools are characterised by their geometric forms, including blades, points, crescents, and triangles, and are usually created through knapping, a process where small, precise flakes are struck off a core. The term "microlith" originates from the Greek words "mikros" (small) and "lithos" (stone), reflecting both their diminutive size and stone composition. These tools were frequently employed as composite tools, hafted onto wooden or bone handles to make spears, arrows, or other implements.

Previous scholars have attempted to define microblades using various criteria, including technological, morphological, and dimensional characteristics. Tixier was the first to classify blades equal to or less than 5 cm in length and under 12 mm in width as "bladelets" (now microblades) (Tixier 1963: 39, 48, 94-96). Subsequently, J.D. Clark characterised microlithic industries as those based on the manufacture of bladelets and flakelets, the maximum length of which does not exceed 50 mm, with the vast majority being under 30 mm long (Clark 1985: 95). These industries are characterised by varying proportions of backed tools and small convex scrapers, which view microblades as "small and thin strips" of rock detached from specially prepared cores through indirect or pressure flaking, approximately 2 mm thick, with parallel sides measuring about 4–7 mm in width and 15–50 mm in length. However, these definitions still exhibit considerable variability, which attracts lithic experts in a global debate (Balter 2010). Regional differences in raw material quality and availability, cultural practices, production skills, and functional requirements contribute to this variability in microblade characteristics, as observed by lithic specialists.

Microlithic Technology in India

The microlithic technology in the Indian subcontinent exhibits considerable regional diversity. For instance, the sites in central India, such as Bhimbetka and Adamgarh, along with those in the western regions like Langhnaj in Gujarat, Bagor in Rajasthan, and Dhaba in Son Valley, are renowned for their rich microlithic assemblages.

These sites provide evidence of a well-developed microlithic tradition featuring various tool types and usage contexts. Sites like Teri in Tamil Nadu, situated in the southern regions, demonstrate a continuity of microlithic technology. Scattered across diverse ecological zones, these sites reflect the widespread adoption of microlithic technology. The development and extensive use of microlithic tools are closely linked to shifts in subsistence strategies. The versatility of microliths enabled prehistoric populations to exploit a range of resources, including small game, fish, and plant materials, ultimately contributing to a population explosion (Misra 2001:491-531).

Microliths

Dantari Hill appears to be a treasure trove of microliths, showcasing a diverse range throughout the site. These microliths, which include blades, flakes, fluted cores, and chips crafted from chert, chalcedony, agate, and quartz, testify to the site's rich diversity. Most notably, the preponderance of microliths consists of blades primarily made from white, red, green, and yellow chert, further emphasising the variety and richness of the Dantari Hill microliths.

Method for Collection of Microliths

Microliths were collected from Dantari Hill in two distinct stages. During the first stage, they were gathered randomly, providing a broad overview of their distribution. A more systematic approach was employed in the second stage by placing a grid at potential locations, enabling a structured and comprehensive collection of tools (Fig. 4.1). Artefacts were collected from the exposed surface of the megaliths through random sample collections. The megalithic cemetery area was divided into various localities, from which microliths were collected from the exposed surface deposits of 23 megalithic burials. This area was further divided into five localities, designated Locality 1 to 5. Locality 4 specifically underwent a systematic collection of tools. To ensure accuracy and precision, a 10 x10 meter grid was laid out, which was further divided into 1 square metre blocks, resulting in 100 blocks within the layout. Each block was meticulously examined and documented (Fig. 4.2). Comprehensive photographs were taken from various angles and corners, capturing the overall pattern of the grids. Close-up pictures of each block, both with and without scale and direction marks, were taken to provide accurate measurements and orientation. Hand drawings were prepared to supplement the visual documentation, offering an additional representation of the site.

Microliths of Dantari Hill

Fig. 4.1. *General view of grids and spatial distribution of lithic assemblages*

Fig. 4.2. *A. General view of the grid layout, B. Close-up view of the grid, C. core and microliths*

Analysis of Randomly Collected Microliths

The main activity involves randomly collecting artefacts from the megalithic burials. The analysis of microliths as artefacts distribution in clusters and burials has been done carefully. Further, the assemblage distribution has also been studied well (Fig. 4.3). In this assemblage, the cores typically have around six blade removals. However, there is one core that produces a maximum of 12 blades. A refined microblade industry has been identified in this locality, where various lengths, widths, and raw preferences can be seen in the final production (Fig. 4.4). Significantly less intact microblades are present in the assemblages, while most microblades are broken. Microblade production in the B-9 locality relied on a highly advanced flaking strategy, as indicated by the sole core. The core comprises a total of 12 intact blade scars, with the absence of any unsuccessful attempt. The production of microlithic tools by the megalithic population of Dantari has involved utilising a variety of chert.

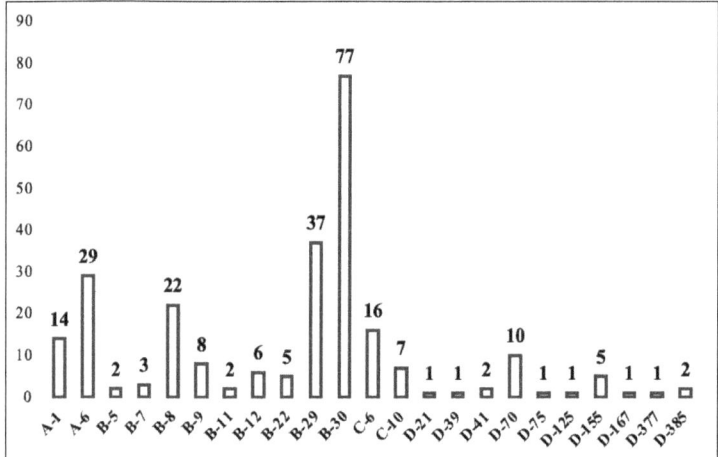

Fig. 4.3. Random collection of microliths from megalithic burials

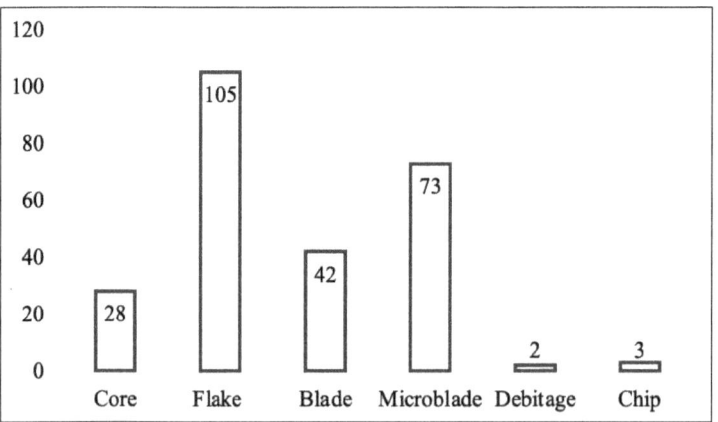

Fig. 4.4. Randomly collected artefacts from Dantari Hill

The assemblage of B-29 comprises only two microblade cores. Both are unidirectional, flaked from almost three sides, and discarded because of the multiple hinge fracture. Locality B-22 has a total absence of a microblade core. Here, only two flake cores have been recovered with few flake removals. Clusters C and D produce a small proportion of lithic specimens compared to preceding assemblages. Assemblages of megalithic cluster C possess a considerable proportion of flake components with a marginal amount of blade and core ingredients. The assemblages from megalith D-75 have only one unidirectional core utilised for microblade production. Cluster 75 of the same megalith produces a single core that flakes unidirectionally from two sides of the prepared platform, showing five blade scars on the core.

The blade and microblade industry of Dantari is affluent and represents a technologically well-developed chain operating system. Blade and microblade components comprise 46% of the entire lithic assemblage of Dantari. Here, it is notable that megalithic clusters A and B only exhibit microblade elements, contributing 41% and 59%, respectively, while all the megalithic burials of Dantari rely on the blade components. Blade and blade fragments of cluster B represent almost three-quarters of the entire assemblage, and the rest of A, C, and D contain 24% collectively (Fig. 4.5).

The lithic core of Dantari shows a range of variability in size and reduction strategies. The alteration of microblade size distribution throughout the localities of megalithic burials has been observed. Both locality A and B megaliths possess some microblade size distribution variability. Megalith A has a maximum microblade length of 1.8 cm, with the majority falling between 1.2 and 0.33 cm. The average length of microblades obtained from clusters A and B is 0.822 cm and 0.796 cm, respectively, while cluster B's

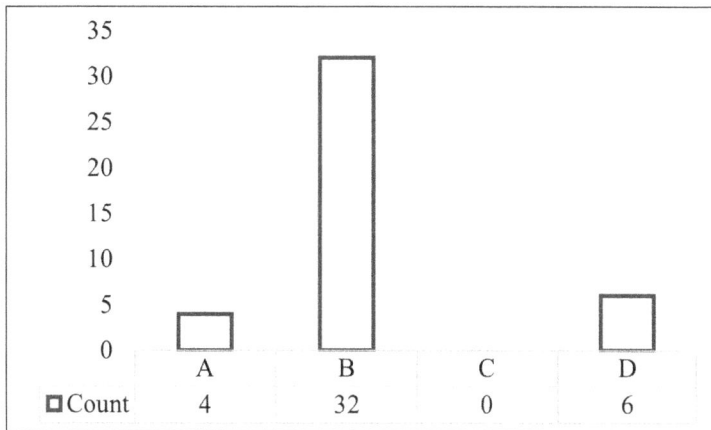

Fig. 4.5. Blade and microblades recovered from the megalithic clusters of Dantari Hill

microblade length distribution intersects between 1.2 and 0.52 cm. In comparison, the mean value for the complete assemblages is 0.811cm (Fig. 4.6a). The dominant core size of this assemblage lies between 2.8 cm and 1.175 cm, while the most extended objective piece is 4.2 cm in length (Fig. 4.6b). Core size analysis indicates a strong correlation between their knapping tactic and length variability. Several cores from this assemblage have been intentionally broken aimed at platform preparation and the production of blade/

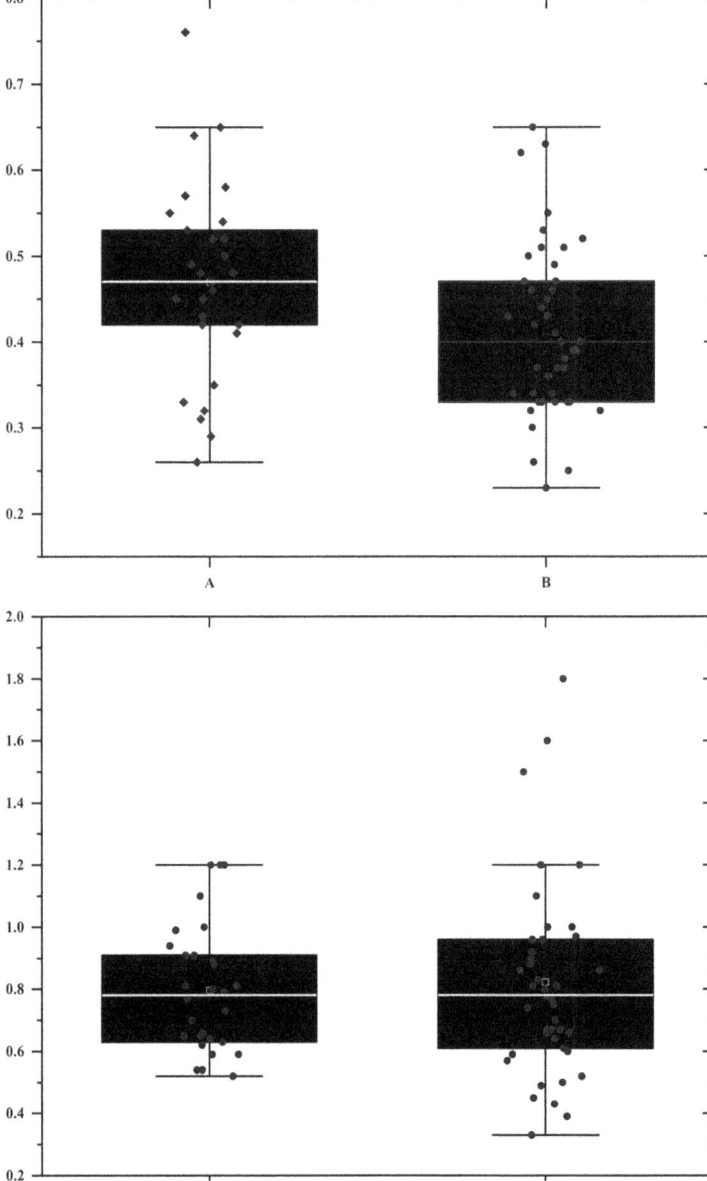

Fig. 4.6.a. Metrical values of width for microblades (A) and cores (B) at Dantari Hill

Fig. 4.6.b. Metrical values of length for microblades (A) and cores (B) at Dantari Hill

bladelets from the pre-utilised and maximised pieces. Several factors, including the raw optimising tendency and functional requirement, conditioned their flaking tradition.

It is essential to mention that almost 95% of the blade assemblage is in broken conditions. The presence of a tiny proportion of intact microblades generates further debate about whether the paleo-landscape of Dantari, which was used as a megalithic burial ground, was also utilised as a factory site for tool production, as indicated by the high concentration of broken blades and by-products in localities. Blade and microblade fragmentation could also result from taphonomic alteration, including wear damage post-depositional processes or collectively both. There could be a hypothetical possibility that the microlithic tools (which are very thin and refined) collected from the megalithic burial context might be grave goods products and later fragmented because of the long-term high depositional pressure.

Analysis of Grid Collection Microliths

The grid area is surrounded by the uplands through scattered chains of hills and situated at 151 meters of Mean Sea Level. Out of 605 artefacts, 49 intact microblades have been spotted in this grid, while the number of cores is 16 (Table 4.1). Techno-typologically, these artefacts are like the random surface collection material of

Table 4.1. Statistics of artifacts in the Dantari grid collection

Sl. No	Block	Artefacts	Fragments	Debitage	Core	Microblade
1	A	15	11	3	0	1
2	B	46	17	20	1	8
3	C	66	20	39	1	6
4	D	79	32	37	4	6
5	E	75	19	46	5	5
6	F	88	26	55	2	5
7	G	100	22	76	1	1
8	H	96	22	64	1	9
9	I	20	3	13	0	4
10	J	20	3	12	1	4
	Total	605	175	365	16	49

the same site (Fig. 4.7). The microblade core of these assemblages was well exploited through advanced production techniques. The site extensively used indirect percussion and pressure knapping for microblade production. Fully prepared platforms have been utilised in numerous cores, while some are partially prepared. This assemblage's most significant number of artefacts belongs to the incomplete section, followed by debitage and fragments. The landscape positions reveal the concentration of artefacts in the blocks. Maximum concentrations of the stone implements were observed between blocks D and H. At the same time, maximum cores are distributed in the middle of the grid between D and F. Notably, the concentration of by-products also lies in the grids of the same blocks.

The H block exhibits a high concentration of microblade elements, followed by B, C, D, E, F, I, J, A & G blocks (Fig. 4.8). This indicates that the prehistoric people possibly used this spot for tool production, conducting finished artefacts and leaving the by-products on the site. Most of the flakes in this assemblage were also found proximally, distally and medially broken. In contrast, the intact detached pieces have more side flakes than elongated ones (Fig. 4.9). The number

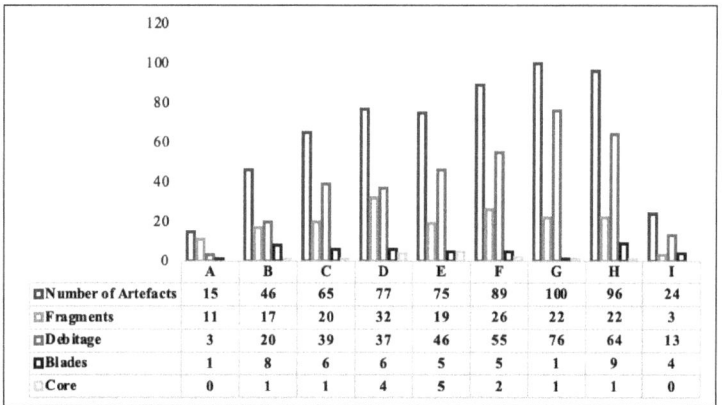

Fig. 4.7. Distribution of artefacts collected from the grid pattern in each block

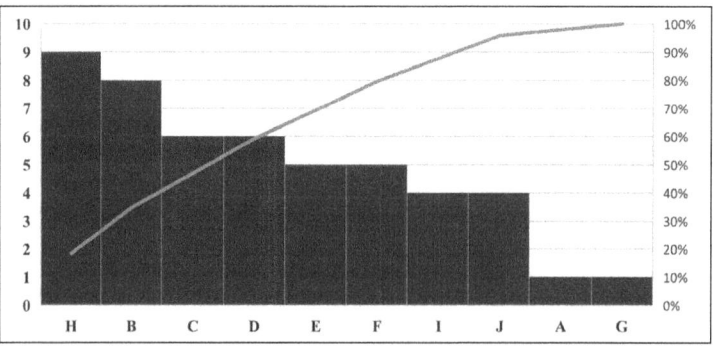

Fig. 4.8. Microblade distribution order, Dantari Hill

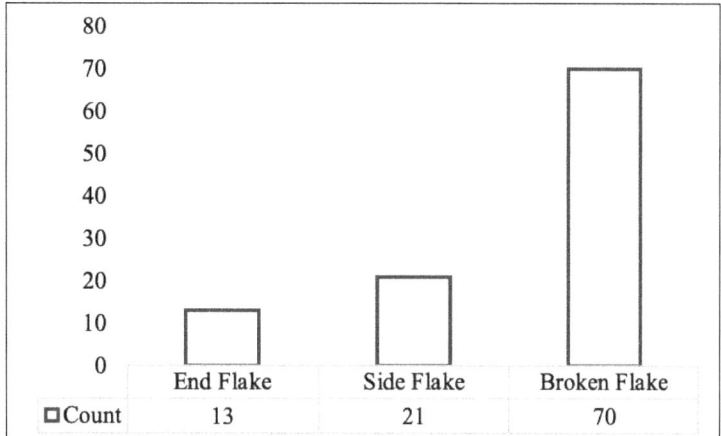

Fig. 4.9. Type of flakes in lithic assemblages of Dantari Hill

of debited items varies in each block. Block G contains the highest number of debitage, followed by blocks H, F, E, C, D, B and A subsequently (Fig 4.10).

Raw Material

The study of raw materials is crucial in analysing prehistoric lithic tools and understanding human technological behaviour, as it provides insights into the selection, procurement, and utilisation of resources by ancient populations. By examining the materials used, researchers can infer trade networks, mobility patterns, and environmental adaptations. Microlith production among the Dantari relies heavily on chert as the primary raw material. However, a few artefacts were crafted from other siliceous materials such as agate and chalcedony. At Dantari, four types of raw materials have been utilised to manufacture microlithic artefacts. These materials are chert, chalcedony, agate, and quartz, with their respective

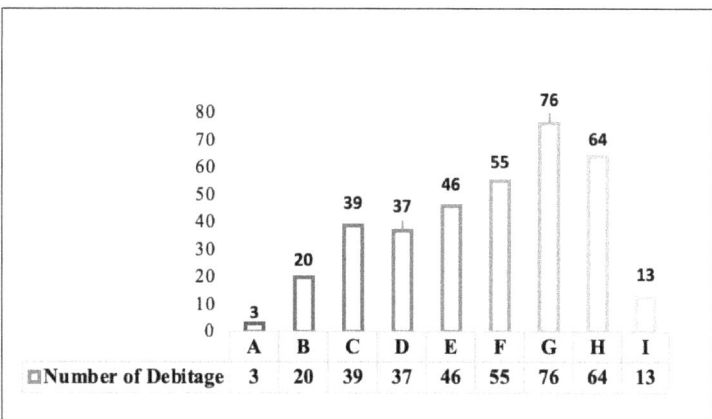

Fig. 4.10. Distribution of debitage in each block

contributions to the assemblage being 90.94%, 2.76%, 4.72%, and 1.57%. The predominance of chert indicates a clear preference for this material in producing microlithic artefacts, followed by agate, chalcedony, and quartz (Fig. 4.11). This preference likely reflects the chert's availability, workability, and suitability for tool-making.

The core exploitation strategy followed here in producing small nodules and chert chunks for systematic microblade production demonstrates the manufacturer's advanced level of technical skill in production technology. Small nodules and chert chunks have been preferred for systematic microblade production. The core exploitation strategy followed here indicates the manufacturer's advanced level of technical skill. Almost all the microblade cores are morphologically wedge-shaped, and removals can be observed from the three sides, whereas one side might be left for the better handgrip during flaking. The assemblages include fluted cores of cylindrical shape with unidirectional removals. The intact microblade from this assemblage exhibits an obscure bulb with a fresh and flat platform. Almost all the microblade cores from this locality are exhausted due to maximum exploitation and seem curated through the advanced pressure knapping technique facilitated by the prepared platform (Fig. 4.12). Several cores from this assemblage were proximally and distally broken for the re-preparation of the platform to maximise the utilisation of the raw material. The findings from Dantari Hill highlight the technological flexibility and behavioural modernity of prehistoric inhabitants. The ability to adapt and innovate in tool production, as evidenced by the advanced microblade manufacturing techniques, reflects a sophisticated level of cognitive and motor skills. The preference for high-quality raw materials and strategically exploiting these resources highlight the community's deep understanding of their local environment.

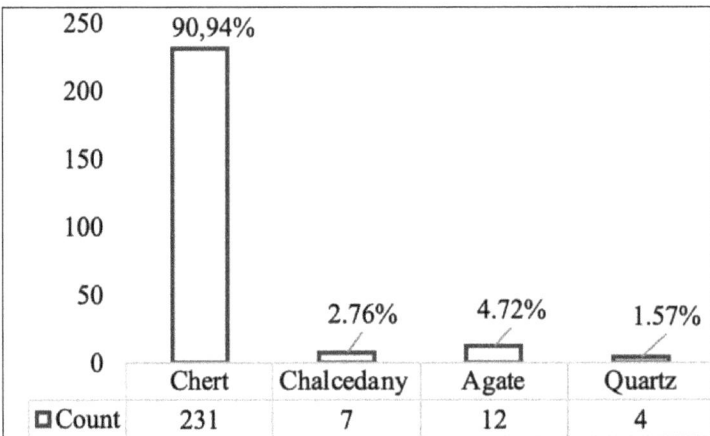

Fig. 4.11. Preference of raw material at Dantari Hill

Microliths of Dantari Hill

Fig. 4.12. Collected microlithic artefacts from Dantari Hill

Discussion

The analysis of the microlithic assemblages offers significant insights into the technological and cultural practices of the megalithic inhabitants of this region. This research highlights several key aspects of their lithic technology, production strategies, and the broader implications for understanding the modernity of behaviour and the adaptability of these ancient communities. The study revealed a remarkable level of techno-typological variability within the microlithic tools. The systematic grid-based collection and subsequent analysis demonstrated a sophisticated understanding and utilisation of local raw materials, predominantly crypto-crystalline siliceous stones such as chert, chalcedony, and agate. The high proportion of chert utilisation underscores its preferred status due to its suitable properties for tool production. Diverse microlithic tools, including flakes, cores, microblades, blades, and debitage, indicate a complex and well-developed lithic technology. The advanced techniques employed for microblade production, such as indirect percussion and pressure knapping, suggest that the inhabitants possessed a high level of technical skill. The systematic preparation of cores, evidenced by the numerous intact and partially prepared platforms, reflects a strategic approach to maximising the efficiency and effectiveness of their tool production.

According to the spatial analysis conducted within the 10x10 metre grid layout, it appears that certain areas were likely engaged in specific activities related to tool production. The concentration of artefacts, particularly in the mid-blocks D to H, suggests that these areas may have been central to lithic manufacturing activities. The distribution pattern, featuring a significant presence of debitage and fragments, supports the hypothesis that Dantari Hill functioned as a factory site for microblade production. Complete reduction sequences, including intact microblades and exhausted cores, further substantiate the idea of in-situ tool production. This finding is crucial as it demonstrates that the site was not merely a habitation or burial ground, but also a significant centre for technological activities. The comprehensive grid collection documentation and analysis clearly show the site's spatial organisation and functional zoning.

Another crucial aspect of this research is the correlation between burial practices and tool production activities. The four identified megalithic clusters (A, B, C, and D) contained various concentrations of artefacts, including lithic tools, as part of the burial goods. This practice suggests a symbolic or practical significance attributed to these tools, possibly reflecting the social or ceremonial aspects of the megalithic community. The variability in microblade size distribution across different clusters (A and B) points to a nuanced understanding of tool utility and possibly different functional roles assigned to these artefacts. The high degree of fragmentation observed in the microblades might be attributed to taphonomic processes or deliberate breakage during tool use or post-depositional activities. Another level of complexity arises when considering the possibility that microliths could be grave goods that undergo fragmentation over time due to long-term pressure, making the interpretation of these assemblages more challenging. While microlithic tools alongside megalithic monuments and rock shelters with paintings indicate a rich cultural landscape where technological, artistic, and ceremonial practices were interwoven. This multifaceted landscape use suggests a complex societal structure capable of sustaining diverse cultural expressions.

Chapter 5
Painted Rock Shelter of Dantari Hill

Sachin Kr. Tiwary, Dheeraj Sharma and Shubham Saurabh

Rock art is understood as representing signs or marks on natural rock surfaces for specific purposes, as practised in ancient societies. This art form includes shapes and symbols etched into caves, rock shelters, and large boulders produced by engraving or scratching the rock or by utilising organic pigments. Rock art may be described as a visual record of human experience and expression made on or with stone, encompassing paintings, drawings, stencils, prints, petroglyphs, engravings, and carvings on various rock surfaces, which in this context represent an essential record of the cultural, religious, and social expressions of early human communities. It is related to human creativity and cognition, for the sophistication of the images reflects the capabilities of the minds behind them. The rock art conveys essential information about belief systems and relationships with the natural environment in prehistoric and early historical societies. Rock art often serves as the primary source of information about ancient cultures, particularly before the advent of written records. Thus, it becomes invaluable for understanding nomadic or semi-nomadic societies that have left minimal material other than their artistic expressions. Rock art exemplifies highly complex cognitive processes, such as symbolism and visual communication, demonstrating that cognitive evolution developed through symbolic thinking.

Previous Work

The second half of the 19th century marked the beginning of studies related to rock art in India. The early discovery of cupules in Almora by Henwood in 1856, although needing more scholarly attention, was a significant milestone (Henwood 1856: 204-205). The subsequent report of rock paintings in Sohagi Ghat by Archibald Carlleyle in 1867 brought the study of rock art in India to the forefront (Carlleyle 1883: 49–55). Carlleyle's discovery was instrumental and served as the impetus for subsequent research in the field. Notably, colonial officers, such as John Cockburn, Alexander Cunningham, Le Mesurier, F. Fawcet, A.H. Francke, and C.A. Silberrad, played a crucial role in recording rock paintings from different parts of India, their contributions forming a significant part of our understanding of this ancient art form.

The district of Mirzapur has a reputation for its comprehensive rock arts, particularly in the Vindhyan region. Part of the much larger Vindhyan rock art zone, it contains many painted rock shelters from Mesolithic times to the historical period. Key sites include Likhunia, Mukhadari, Borgaon, and Lakhma, which represent a variety of pictographs covering anthropomorphic and zoomorphic figures and geometrical designs, as well as activities connected with daily life and rituals (Tewari 1990). Hunting and dancing art were found, while later, historical elements of horse riders and wheeled vehicles reflected a long-lasting artistic tradition (Varma 2012; Neumayer 2013). Considerable contributions to the research of the Mirzapur rock art were made, and documentations were carried out since the 1970s by Yashodhar Mathpal, together with quite functional analyses of artistic styles and cultural contexts by Mathpal (1984). Erwin Neumayer has done complete research on Indian rock art, with some data of great value about Mirzapur, enabling insight into the chrono-cultural value represented at these sites (Neumayer 2013). The work of Radha Kant Varma in the area is also significant for understanding the Mesolithic age of Mirzapur and rock art (Varma 1986, 1984). Systematic surveys and excavations by Rakesh Tewari in the area correlated the rock art with the archaeological finds, mainly for a more precise chronology (Tewari 2013:381-388). The ethnoarchaeological research in Chunar by Ajay Pratap has contributed much to the acknowledgement of connections between ancient rock art and the current tribal artistic forms, greatly enriching our knowledge concerning the creative tradition of this region (Pratap 2024). These studies further highlight the importance of Mirzapur in the broader context of Indian rock art and provide insights into the prehistoric life and artistic traditions of North-Central India.

Location of the Shelter

The painted rock shelter is located on the eastern edge of the hill at 25.0215 N, 82.91563 E (Fig. 5.1). Paintings are found in only one of the six rock shelters at the site. This rock shelter measures 25 metres in length from north to south, with a maximum height of 6.3 metres above ground level and two distinct levels (Fig. 5.2). It faces east and southeast, providing a view of the Jargo Dam (Fig. 5.3). The pictographs on the ceiling and walls distinguish it from the others.

Methodology

Detailed measurements were conducted for the micro-documentation of the painted rock shelter, which was divided from bottom to top

Painted Rock Shelter of Dantari Hill

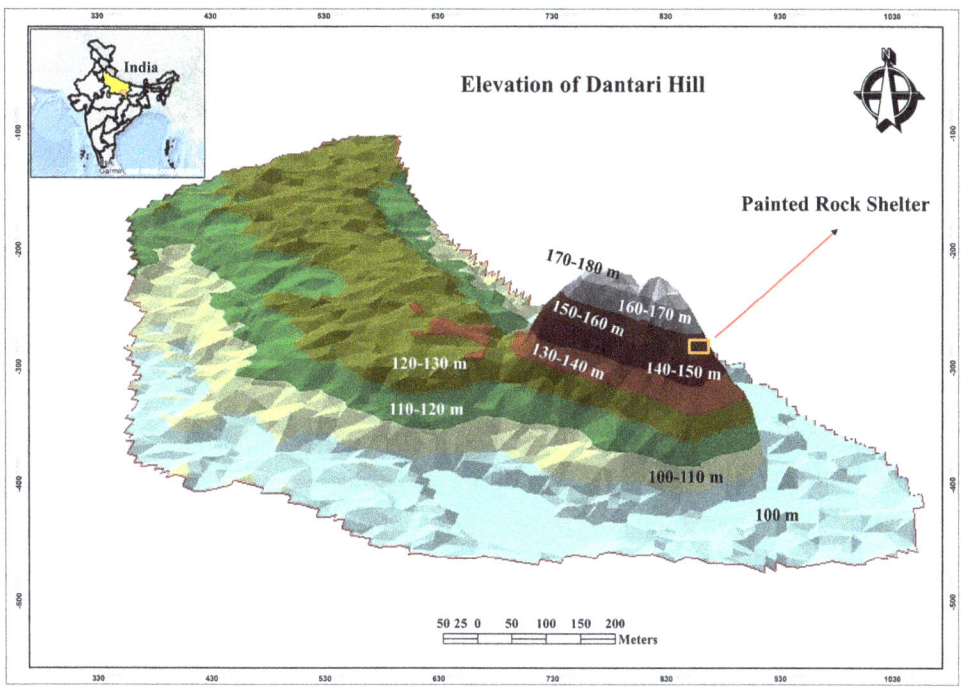

Fig. 5.1. Location map of painted rock shelter

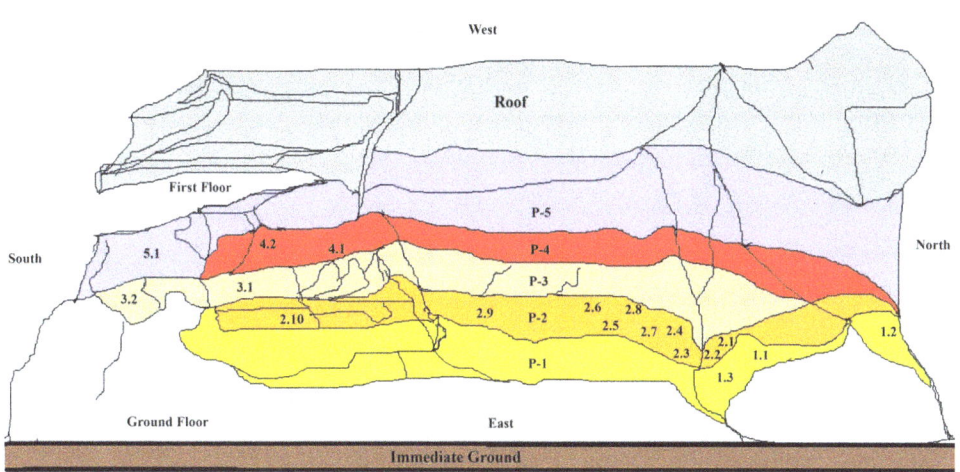

Fig. 5.2. Line drawing of the five different panels and clusters

into five panels based on the visible layers, labelled P-1 to P-5. Furthermore, each of these panels was subdivided into clusters of paintings: Panel 1 contained 3 clusters, Panel 2 contained 10 clusters, Panel 3 contained 2 clusters, Panel 4 contained 2 clusters, and Panel 5 contained 1 cluster. Each panel, cluster, and individual painting was measured and photographed, totalling more than 100 executions. The data is organised in an extensive database that catalogues every

Fig. 5.3. General view of the shelter along with the Jargo dam

execution, providing details and characteristics of each panel, cluster, and painting. The database includes photographs, sketches, thematic analyses, and spatial contexts.

Micro-Documentation of the Execution and the Shelter

Panel 1: War Scene and Faunal Cluster

This panel is divided into three parts, each dealing with a different theme. The themes are generally related to the day-to-day life and historical context of the period depicted. Below are detailed descriptions of the themes.

1a) Panel 1.1

This cluster of panels, measuring 68x50 cm in size, is located on the north side of the shelter, and all the painted figures face left towards the south. The scene shows a war theme with energetic images of horse riders and galloping animals in movement. The first image is a male horse rider painted in dark ochre facing east and measures 16x13 cm

Painted Rock Shelter of Dantari Hill

(Fig. 5.4). He has a barbed spearhead on his right and a bridle on his left, with a dagger worn at his waist; the head is cone-shaped. In this galloping attitude, the man on the horse's forelock is very distinct, with an open mouth and a tail represented by two main lines with three brush strokes, giving further expression to movement. The second figure is also oriented east and painted in dark ochre, depicting another horse rider of about 17x15 cm. This rider holds a bow and arrow with his right hand and a bridle with his left. Like the first rider, he is also equipped with a dagger at his waist and a conical head. The horse is also in a running or galloping pose with noticeable ears on the forelock and an open mouth. The tail is again rendered with two primary lines and three strokes of a brush. Surprisingly, the horse's breast is pierced with two arrows to add drama to the situation. The third and the fourth forms of galloping animals are also oriented to the east, painted in dark ochre. The third figure measures 12 x 7 cm, and the fourth is 13 x 8 cm. Due to erosion, it is not easy to recognise the upper front portions of these animals, but they must belong to horses since they are similar in appearance to the first two figures. Their tails and ears still show up to some extent, enhancing the clustering effect to create a dynamic composition for these animals.

1b) Panel 1.2

This panel is situated 50 cm below cluster 1.1 and measures 13x8 cm. It features a south-facing animal figure painted in light ochre. Erosion

Fig. 5.4. Horse riders with weapons in the panel 1.1 (D-Stretch)

has reached the lower part of the figure, though the horns or ears can still be seen.

1c) Panel 1.3: Inscription

This panel, measuring 141 x 52 cm in size, lies below cluster 1.2 and contains an inscription in Devanagari script, painted in dark ochre. The text is four lines long; it is partly eroded, and only fragments remain, including phrases such as "*Rama Sakala,*" "*Soogreeva.*", "*Seeva Charana.*", and "*La Sutana* (?)" The inscription adds a textual layer to this visual narrative.

Panel 2: Diverse Imagery

This panel represents a diversity of scenes of human and animal figures with inscriptions. It is remarkable for its broad diversity of representations, which range from warriors to animals and ritualistic-geometric symbols to representations, expressed in different colours and styles. This panel surface is worn, with exfoliation and erosion processes that make it difficult to interpret. The themes are described below.

2a) Panel 2.1

This panel has several anthropomorphic and faunal representations, inscriptions, and unknown figures. The size is 381x107 cm, with an orientation towards the east. It represents some scenes from war to nature, all in dark ochre. The rock sedimentation of the shelter is very apparent, while the surface is undulated with large exfoliation, that has caused partial erosion to many figures. The panel has four distinct superimpositions, differentiated by differences in taphonomy, hue, style, and execution techniques. These superimpositions range from off-white in Phase I to light ochre in Phase II, dark red or brown in Phase III and light red painted scripts in Phase IV. The panel's left side is crowded with human forms, most of which are armed; the right has few figures. Thin and thick brushstrokes are both used in the drawing.

2b) Panel 2.2:

This panel is located 10 cm below panel 2.1, measures 60 × 20 cm, and faces south. The surface is undulating and exfoliated, with a white calcium carbonate coating that masks the figures. Due to this erosion, anthropogenic representations have become visible with D-stretch analysis in a delivery scene depicting a woman in childbirth. The two rows of figures are considerably faded and blurred, with only a few human figures being vaguely discernible. Prominent among them is the tall standing figure, with arms flexed at the elbows, resembling a "T", similar to the punch-marked coins. Another distinctive figure is the small human rendered in thick strokes.

2c) Panel 2.3:

This panel is situated, at an angle to the west, about 10 cm away from panel 2.2. It is oriented to the south and measures 30x60 cm. Its surface is undulated and eroded, with very faded figures. D-stretch analysis identifies several human figures in different postures, although only five can be identified.

2d) Panel 2.4:

This panel is 80x30 cm facing south and located to the left of panel 2.3. The condition of the surface of this panel is highly weathered and eroded, which has caused segregation in sedimentary rock blocks. In the scene, there is a horizontal single-line of twelve human figures; the figure at the extreme right of the line is like "A" and "X." Above the human figures, there is a hollow cross with a taurine or *Chakra*, with a *Trishula* symbol inside, similar to some signs on the early historic punch-marked coins. The panel includes a thin line that zigzags and represents the human figures, contributing to another stylistic solid element.

2e) Panel 2.5:

This panel is 110x30 cm in size. It is situated to the left of panel 2.4 and below the wall panel 2.6. The surface is undulating and exfoliating, with a partial coating of white calcium carbonate obscuring the figures. The figures are in poor condition and eroded, hence, difficult to recognise, but an analysis with D-stretch shows the probable presence of a domestication scene along the extreme left and right edges of the panel. There is also a ritualistic scene with palm prints, unknown figures, and a human figure standing above some animal. The animal species, however, is not easily recognizable, for it has some of the characteristics of an elephant, like the trunk, tusk, and tail.

2f) Panel 2.6:

This panel is located just above panel 2.5 and measures 81x34 cm. It contains a Devanagari script inscription within an outline heart: "*Sugreeva Laal Heero*" and "*Neelamee Heeroin*," done in dark ochre.

Pre and Protohistoric Archaeology of Chunar, Mirzapur (Uttar Pradesh)

2g) Panel 2.7:

This panel is situated to the left of panel 2.5 and measures 15x20 cm; it faces south. The condition is similar to that of panel 2.2, with undulations and erosion affecting the figures' visibility. This panel has two representations of anthropogenic beings (Fig. 5.5). One resembles the human figure in panel 2.2. Another domestication scene is where a human figure is placed beside an animal. The style, at least in this respect, is uniform with the other panels and uses dark ochre.

2h) Panel 2.8:

This panel is to the left of panel 2.6 and above panel 2.7. It measures 30 x 16 cm and faces east. This panel is significantly damaged, as soot marks indicate it was subjected to fire. Even in this condition, an inscription in the Devanagari script is present, along with a vertical line drawing that could not be identified.

2i) Panel 2.9:

This panel, 18x22 cm, is located to the left of panel 2.8 and bears six faunal figures; all are faded and cannot be identified. On the angular face of the shelter, there is also a flower depicted in dark ochre.

Fig. 5.5. Human figure along with animal showing domestication scene (D-Stretch)

2j) Panel 2.10:

The last panel is situated on the left side of panel 2.9, oriented east, and measures 30x32 cm. The erosion is fair, and two superimpositions can be observed. The first layer is yellowish, while the second is dark red. The anthropomorphic depicted includes two human figures in yellow and one in red. Although these figures are still distinguishable, there are several other additional faded executions around the panel.

Panel 3: Complex Ceilings

This panel, located on the shelter's ceiling, consists of a mixture of human, animal, and geometric figures. Unique in its placement, it represents complicated artistic techniques for that time with its red and yellow pigments. Of importance are the detailed finger-painted figures and geometric patterns that reflect the rich cultural narrative of that time. Below is a detailed description of the themes of panel 3.

3a) Panel 3.1:

This panel, oriented towards the south, measures 40x32 cm and consists of various anthropomorphic, faunal, geometric, and unidentified figures. Most of the artwork is rendered in dark red pigment, although some figures (mainly anthropomorphic) are highlighted in yellow. A notable characteristic is the substantial amount of thickly applied pigment, evident on a standing human figure measuring 8x7 cm. Despite some damage at the top, the figure remains quite distinct, and the algae covering it suggests that it has been exposed to the environment for an extended period. Additionally, there are eight different strokes of fingers, varying in shape and length, measuring 10x4 cm, showing a worn appearance indicative of rubbing and modification or erosion. Another animal figure, created using fingers, enhances the panel's tactile texture, being partially visible and measuring 12x9 cm.

The other figures, of unknown identity, are 6x6 cm and 8x8 cm, both in dark red colour, and their ambiguous forms add to the enigmatic quality of the panel. At the bottom right of the open-armed human figure is a geometric symbol, *damaru*-shaped and drawn with thin lines, probably with a fine brush, which measures 3.2x2 cm and brings an abstract element into the panel. Another very striking figure is that of another human figure 10x7 cm and done in yellow, which is shown in an open-armed attitude, suggesting the letter "W." The slender waist and the hair sticking straight up on this figure, as seen in rock paintings from ISKO rock shelter in Hazaribagh, Jharkhand, indicate a possible cultural or style relationship. Another important geometrical pattern on the panel is a 22x22 cm square with circles at each corner. This square-shaped pattern has a diagonal square with circles at its corners and a central circle. This depth-defining intricate geometrical design is located on the right side of the demur-shaped symbol and below the human figure described above.

3b) Panel 3.2:

This panel is situated on the ceiling, 204 cm south of panel 3.1; it measures 40x25 cm and represents probably a burial scene. The picture was placed within a narrow cavity in the rock, 204 cm above panel 3.1, while the ceiling only sat 32 cm above the level of the rock's floor, and thus the artist lay down when painting. The burial scene comprises four human figures surrounded by 39 thick dots. Although these figures are arranged as two couples, they seem to hold hands, which might be a ritualistic element of their burial. The execution is both in thick and thin strokes, and the head of the figures is covered with tiny dots, which would seem to point to the megalithic tradition. This drawing of a circle burial at a cairn is part of a larger context of ritualistic and funerary art in ancient Indian rock shelters. The anthropomorphic figures, geometric patterns, and ritualistic scenes, all combined in panels 3.1 and 3.2, provide a narrative of comprehensive expression of the life of prehistoric times, its belief system, artistic practices, and inextricable linking between the human and spiritual realms in ancient cultures.

Panel 4: War and Geometric Scenes

This panel has two themes: dynamic war and geometrical symbols. On one half, there is a vivid scene of combat with meticulous depictions of warriors, and on the other, symbolic geometrical figures of possible ritual or ceremonial significance. Contrasted with both style and subject, it gives a full view of that time's artistic and ritualistic practices. Below is a detailed description of the themes of panel 4.

4a) Panel 4.1:

Panel 4.1 is 77x100 cm in size and oriented southeast, with a lively war scene executed in very dark red paint. It comprises three horizontal lines depicting battle or combat scenes. Like the topography in panel 2.2, there are over twenty figures. Still, only six are recognisably distinguished with D-Stretch technology (Fig. 5.6). In the front line, a horseman figure turned to the right and carried a sword in his

Painted Rock Shelter of Dantari Hill

raised right hand. Facing left, in front of the rider, another warrior is stringing a big bow and arrow. The two figures are done in a thick line, making them vivid. The figure of the warrior with the bow and arrow is in a stick pattern, reflecting simplicity and clarity. A second standing warrior figure, 9x13 cm in size, was holding a sword in his right hand at the extreme right side of the panel. Another figure nearby holding a sword is a little smaller, with dimensions of 10x6 cm in size.

The following line incorporates a more complex war scene, 81x14 cm, where the warriors hold swords and shields. Several faded paintings are not so easily identified. One is executed in a thick brush technique: a warrior with a sword in his right hand and a shield in his left. His body is filled in, and he comes more to the foreground of the panel. The second figure is a human standing with a posture in one of his hands, similar to the burial figures mentioned in previous panels. However, it has eroded from the middle down, so seeing the rest is impossible. The third line, 42x22 cm in size, details a war scene in which six warrior figures and two others cross each other, making them hardly recognisable. It contains two warrior groups fighting each other. This group on the left is rendered in a different style, with thick stick patterns and, very prominent, an emphasis on the feet. Two warriors face towards the right and take stringing positions with bows and arrows, while one warrior stands between them, holding a sword with a shield (Fig. 5.7).

Fig. 5.6: General view of the panel 4.1. (D-Stretch)

Fig. 5.7. Warrior scene with bows, arrows, sword and shield of panel 4.1.

This is nearly at the opposite end of the other group, with a warrior fighting hand to hand, overlapping figures, and carrying a sword in his left hand and a shield in his right. In the middle of this group, one figure is larger than all the others, holding a shield in his right hand with a sword in his left. There is a sheath at his waist to a valorous blade and an arrow piercing his shield to show that the battle is fierce. The head of this well-known warrior is indicated by a thick dot, thus signifying that he might be the head. Slightly at the back of this central figure is another warrior with a large shield and sword. The differences noted in this group from the first are less prominent feet, their bodies rendered in thick strokes, and most carry shields and swords.

4b) Panel 4.2:

Panel 4.2, above panel 4.1 facing the southeast, is 40x40 cm. The panel shows some geometric scenes with dark red pigment figures. The main figure is *pataka* or *sthambha* (pillar)-like in appearance, as visible in some of the early Indian coins, especially when enclosed by railings. The size of this figure, 34x6 cm, is like an erected post and perhaps represents something ceremonial or architectural. On either side of the post, geometric symbols like a triangle and an arrow flank the central figure. These symbols, 10x10 cm each, introduce into this scene a feature of abstraction and may stand for directional markers or other symbolic elements in the bigger context of the imagery.

Painted Rock Shelter of Dantari Hill

Panel 5: Anthropomorphic and Geometric Clusters

This panel represents the human form and geometric symbols. Although visibility has been compromised by surface coating in places, enhanced images make it clear that human forms and abstract symbols are portrayed. These symbols bring forth symbolic and ritualistic aspects of the culture depicted. Below is a detailed description of the themes of panel 5.

5a) Panel 5.1:

Panel 5.1, east-facing and 130x68 cm in size, is located on the southern face of the ceiling in the first story of a double-storied rock shelter (Fig. 5.8). The surface of this panel is undulating and covered with a white calcium carbonate coating, percolated from the top of the rock, which masks parts of the figures and makes identification a little difficult. Nonetheless, D-Stretch enhancement has made seven figures on the panel visible, two of which are precise human figures, with the other two being geometric symbols. The figure, executed using a thick brush and with geometric patterns, has a well-defined left hand, with the right hand partially obscured by what could have been superimposition. The fingers of the left hand are well differentiated, while the figure's phallus and legs are of equal length and thickness. Two strokes across the top of the head indicate that he is wearing some headgear while his upper body is much broader than the lower part, making this image essentially

Fig. 5.8. General and close view (D-Stretch) of the panel 5 in the rectangular shape

geometric. The second image of a human done with a thick brush is similar in style to the first one but measures 4x3 cm. It is also partially covered with a white coating of calcium carbonate. The geometric symbols on this panel include two clear patterns of triangles, one 3x3 cm and one 4x4 cm. Each triangle has a stroke from its apex down, center-wise, as if it depicted a vulva symbol. These symbols represent an abstraction in the symbolism of the anthropomorphic figures, as they likely capture some cultural or ritual aspect.

Analysis

The minute documentation of five panels at Dantari Hill provides an interesting and fresh perspective on understanding the creative expressions found there (Fig. 5.9). The location of paintings on this set of panels seems to have a certain purpose, as they have been done to tell a certain type of story or maybe a concept.

Documenting the colours utilised in this shelter (Fig. 5.10) will deepen our understanding of the ancient painters' artistic choices and symbolic meanings. Various paintings point to their colour schemes, which give clues to their subjects, narratives, and cultural contexts that they represent. Dark and light ochre, easily available on Dantari Hill in large hematite stone and white from locally available limestone, bespeaks some choice in deliberately using materials. The meaning given to different colours could be profound. For example, white, used to represent a megalithic burial, may symbolise purity and transcendence or underline the monumentality of the element described. In both ways, the style harmonises the background and unites the artwork with its surroundings. Indeed, precisely the same use of white for burial symbols occurs in the rock art of Tamilnadu, perhaps testifying to cultural or symbolic continuity.

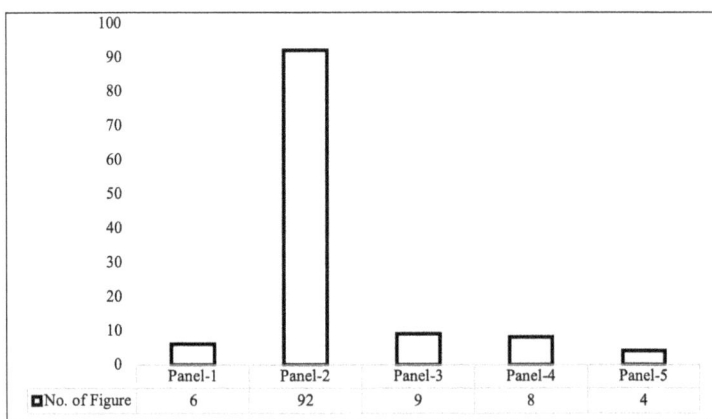

Fig. 5.9. Panel-wise distribution of the rock painting, Dantari Hill

Fig. 5.10. Colour-wise distribution of the rock painting, Dantari Hill

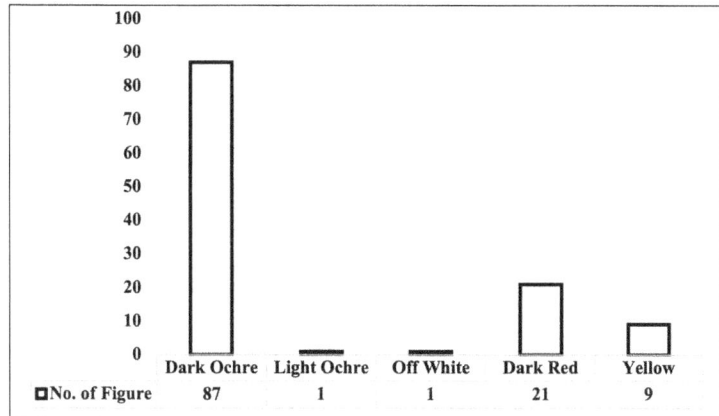

Significantly, the orientation of the rock painting facing towards the cardinal direction portrays deliberate placement within nature (Fig. 5.11). Indeed, such alignment could supply information regarding the intentions of the ancient artist, his interaction with the environment, and possible symbolic meanings. In most cases, they have faced south, which indicates a connection between the artwork and the southern scenery. This orientation probably relates to the appreciation of the view, including the source of water, the movement of wildlife, and the general beauty of the southern landscape. The association with the source of water itself stresses practical considerations that early man not only depended on but also appreciated in terms of aesthetics and functionality.

Placing rock paintings at a specified height (Fig. 5.12) above the immediate ground level provides valuable insights into the intentions and perspectives of the painters. This could be the artists' personal viewpoint or "eye level" and thus could be a creative decision. This position of the paintings may indicate an attempt to dignify or revere the pictures. Strategically placing the paintings at a specific height

Fig. 5.11. Orientation-wise distribution of the rock painting, Dantari Hill

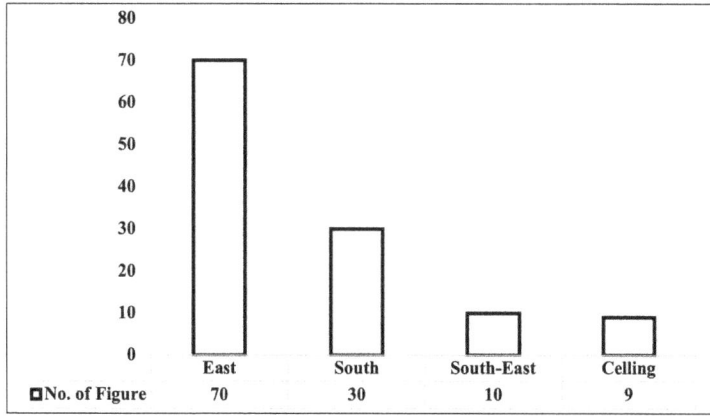

Fig. 5.12. Rock painting executed on different heights (in cm) Dantari Hil

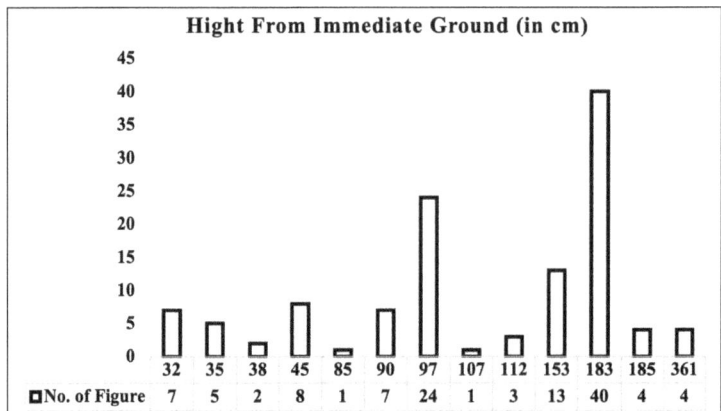

likely draws more attention to them, increasing their perceived importance by better integrating them within the site's surroundings and enhancing their sense of value and purpose.

The depiction of rock art found at different heights in the shelter is well shown through the graphs (Fig. 5.13). The rock paintings are immensely diverse, with scenes, objects, and symbols that befit the complexity and depth of the artistic expressions of this site. The frequent appearance of human figures indicated a strong interest in depicting human activities and presence. These figures symbolise everyday life, cultural traditions, rituals, or abstract ideas. Since they are depicted, the horses probably symbolise something about movement, power, and status, for horses generally do not form part of the usual motifs. The image of horse riders underscores some equestrian roles that

Fig. 5.13. Scene-wise distribution of the rock painting, Dantari

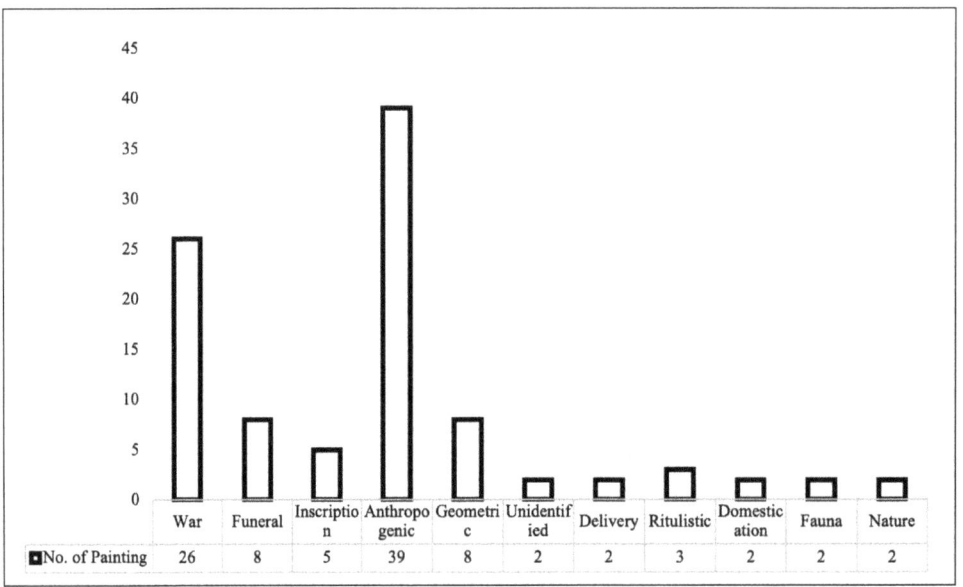

Painted Rock Shelter of Dantari Hill

consequently impart the meaning of their status as warriors, leaders, or important people. Moreover, it can be understood from the war scenes shown in the paintings that conflict and fights were a part of the ancient civilisation and thus what their artistic expression regarding the war scenarios and associated cultural beliefs has been. Only one megalithic burial has been shown, symbolising some customs, traditions or beliefs associated with death and life after death.

Megalithic Burial Depiction

The presence of megalithic burial depiction in the rock art of Dantari introduces an exciting dimension to the site's archaeology. The work, placed amidst several megalithic structures, has the effect of intersecting artistic and monumental elements. Connected with funerary or ceremonial practices, the megaliths find a space in the painting, which possibly holds certain symbolic meanings concerning these activities. That would make placing the painting amongst the megaliths one in an area specially set aside for ritual or ceremonial purposes, providing that personal link between the art and the megaliths themselves (Fig. 5.14).

This suggests a communicative purpose for the painting, perhaps even carrying some important message, or narrative. In our interpretation,

Fig. 5.14. Megalithic burial depiction at Dantari Hill

we suggest that the painting is one of battle and heroism and the preserved memories of the dead, against which would be the ancient customs of memorialising lost warriors. Megaliths and artwork could connote a ceremonial or commemorative function, where the painting would have amplified the importance of the rituals. As manifested in Dantari Hill, the coexistence of these two aspects gives a rich understanding of the ancient inhabitants' cultural and symbolic practices.

Discussion

Dantari Hill, with its elevated position, provides a strategic view of the surrounding landscape, easy access to water, and plentiful natural resources. The megalithic burials and rock art indicate that the people likely utilised these elements for symbolic or ceremonial purposes. The rock paintings, especially on the hill's southern side, have been selected for their scenic backdrop, adding spiritual and aesthetic dimensions to the artwork. The area's abundant natural resources, including minerals for pigments and a reliable water supply, catered to the daily needs of early settlers. Employing megaliths for burial rituals suggests that the site held symbolic value that extended beyond its practical advantages. The coexistence of rock art and megaliths emphasises the site's multifaceted role in ancient life, possibly serving as a central location for rituals and cultural gatherings. The deliberate use of colours in the paintings, such as bright ochre for spiritual themes, dark ochre for scenes of daily life, and white for religious significance and so on, perhaps indicates that the artists selected their palette with intent, aiming to convey specific themes and emotions. The orientation of the paintings may guide the viewer through a visual narrative, unveiling cultural or symbolic messages. The alignment of the paintings with the artist's height suggests a more personal connection between the artwork and the viewer, reflecting the artist's perspective. The choice of rock surfaces and the height of the paintings likely influenced how the art was perceived and engaged with. In summary, the megalithic paintings at Dantari Hill offer valuable insights into the complex cultural practices of the past. They reflect a sophisticated society engaged in daily life, conflict, spiritual beliefs, and artistic expression. The integration of megaliths and rock art enriches our understanding of how ancient peoples intertwined their creativity with their environment and monumental structures, revealing the richness of their cultural and symbolic practices.

Chapter 6
Archaeology of Chunar: Megaliths, Microliths and Rock Paintings

Dheeraj Sharma, Deepesh Singh and Virag G. Sontakke

The geophysical location of Chunar has always played a vital role in shaping the archaeological landscape of Vindhya. Its proximity to the fertile alluvial tracts of the Ganges and the abundance of resources in the Vindhya have remained chief factors for human beings for a long time. Recent survey in Chunar uncovered several archaeological sites that testify to the rich cultural heritage of the area. A comprehensive survey of the region was conducted to explore the megalithic cemeteries, painted rock shelters, microlithic sites, and habitation areas (Fig. 6.1). Each site was meticulously documented, highlighting unique characteristics and significance to understand the nature of the location and its interconnections. These findings provide valuable insights into the cultural and historical landscape of the region.

Previous Work

Sir Alexander Cunningham was the first to map this region in the archaeological world. During his exploration in 1861-62, he identified several cairns and stone circles in Chunar (Cunningham 1871: 30-31). As per Cunningham's findings, the distribution of megalithic burials extended across a substantial expanse, ranging from Ramsarovar and Jargo Dam in the northern region to Chudia Hill in the southern part. This area covered an estimated distance spanning approximately 11 to 16 km. After Cunningham, Le Mesurier reported megalithic monuments in the hilly area of the south Chunar. He wrote a letter to Arthur Grote on October 24th 1867, mentioning approximately 100 cairns or barrows in the hilly region near Chunar contained perfect kist or cist (Mesurier 1867: 164-166). Upon opening one of these cairns, Le Mesurier uncovered teeth or jaw bones. He also sketched the cairn and a map of where these cairns (tumuli) were spread. This was the first official report of Megalithic burials in the Vindhyan region. Subsequently, Archibald Campbell Carlleyle, in 1883, while a survey in the hilly tract of Chunar, discovered sepulchral mounds, cairns, rock cave paintings, and stone implements (Carlleyle 1883: 49-55).

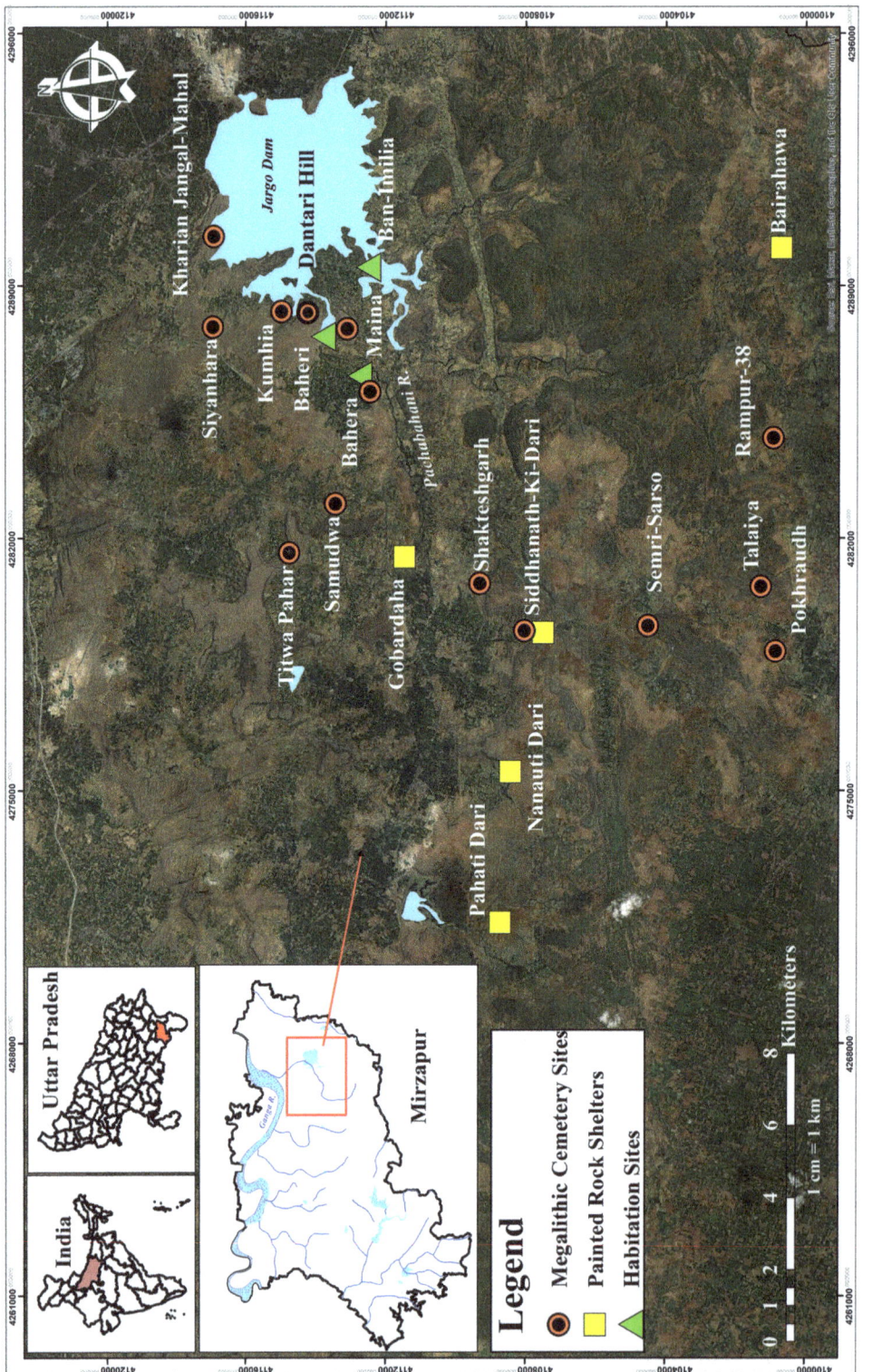

Fig. 6.1: Distribution of archaeological sites in Chunar, Mirzapur, Uttar Pradesh

In the post-independence period, Banaras Hindu University undertook an expansive survey of this region. In the 1960s, the late Professor P. C. Pant conducted excavations, unearthing five megalithic burials that enriched our understanding of the cultural and funerary practices prevalent in the area (Pant 1985: 481-484). Several investigations by U.P. State Archaeology and Banaras Hindu University were conducted after the 1990s (IAR 1990-91: 75). In the same duration, Rakesh Tewari carried out an extensive study and found numerous sites in Chunar. He conducted a comprehensive village-to-village survey on Rajgarh block, revealing multiple cultural sites. The findings included pottery types such as NBPW, black slipped ware, red ware, black ware, black-and-red ware, and grey ware, spanning from the 6th century BCE to the Medieval period (Tewari 1997: 51-58; 1999: 163-223).

Moreover, Chunar has been a significant source of sandstone since ancient times. P.C. Pant and Vidula Jayaswal traced an ancient quarry site of the Mauryan period. They identified over 300 quarry sites near Chunar, where the Ashokan pillars were carved (Pant and Jayaswal 1990: 49-52). Additionally, many scholars have explored this region, uncovering several archaeological sites (Kumar 2022; Pratap 2016; Tewari 1990: 51-58). These findings highlight Chunar's rich archaeological heritage and underscore its importance in understanding ancient history.

Megalithic Cemetery Sites

The southern region of Chunar is characterised by numerous small hills, many of which contain megalithic cemeteries. Detailed micro-documentation was carried out at each site, recording key information such as the number of cemeteries, their geographical coordinates, dimensions, photographs, and current conditions. These meticulous records provide a comprehensive understanding of the megalithic sites in the area. The details of these megalithic sites in Chunar are as follows.

Maina Pahar (25.01388, 82.90767)

The megalithic cemetery site of Maina Pahar is located 17 km southeast of the Chunar tehsil. It lies 350 metres south of Dantari Hill, across the Pachbahani River. The megalithic burials at Maina Pahar are constructed on a rocky outcrop that remains uncultivated. A survey of the site uncovered 171 megalithic burials of various types, with cairns and cists within cairns being the most prevalent. A single independent menhir is also present, measuring 95×88×22 cm (Fig. 6.2). The diameters of the cairns range from 3 to 18 metres; 87 burials have a circumference of less than 5 m, with an average deposit varying from 10 cm to 1.40 metres. Contemporary stone quarries have damaged many megalithic structures, and locals have unearthed several burial sites in search of treasure from these ancient cemeteries (Fig. 6.3).

Titwa Pahar (25.03027, 82.84526)

Titwa Pahar is situated approximately ten kilometres southwest of Chunar tehsil. The site is situated in an appropriate location where small hills encircle the megalithic cemetery on three sides and water bodies on the other, giving it a promising appearance. Titwa Pahar is a small hillock containing 31 megalithic burials. While megalithic remains are typically located on the slope of a hill, a few have been identified at the top. Cairns represent the most significant type of megaliths at this site (Fig. 6.4). Their diameters range from 5 to 15 metres, with an average deposit of 50 cm to 1.50 meters above the surface (Fig. 6.5).

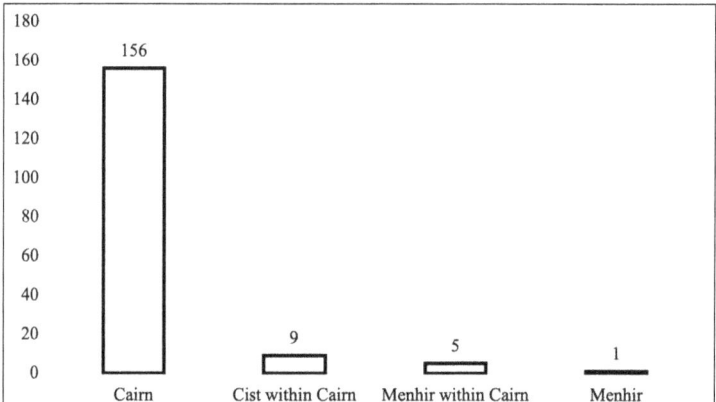

Fig. 6.2. Distribution of megalithic burials at Maina Pahar

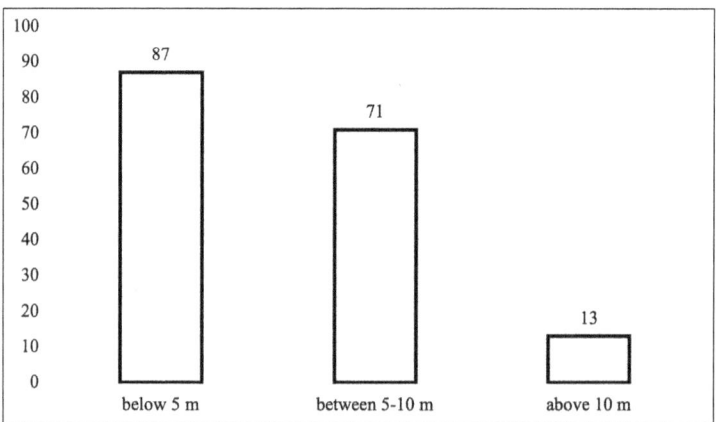

Fig. 6.3. Size variations of megaliths at Maina Pahar

Fig.6.4. Distribution of megalithic burials at Titwa Pahar

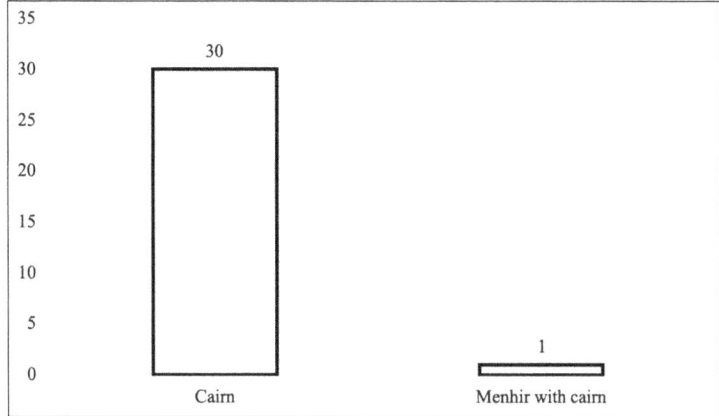

Fig.6.5. Size variations of megalithic burials at Titwa Pahar

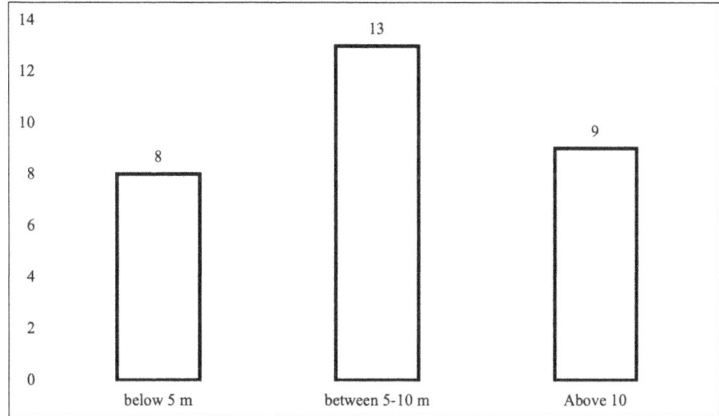

Shakteshgarh (24.98043; 82.8356)

The megalithic cemetery site of Shakteshgarh is about 22 km southwest of Chunar tehsil. Megalithic burials are primarily located on the slope of the hill. A detailed survey of the cemetery yielded approximately 50 megalithic burials. Cairns and Menhir within cairns are the most significant megalithic types at this site (Fig. 6.6). Their diameter varied between 5 and 15 meters, with an average deposit of 30 cm to 1.50 meters above the surface. Menhirs are usually erected at the southern portion with an average height of 1 to 1.5 meters (Fig. 6.7). Most megaliths are in disturbed conditions due to stone quarries and human interventions.

Bahera (25.008278, 82.88998)

Bahera is situated 17 kilometres south of the Chunar tehsil in the Mirzapur district. The megalithic burial site lies three kilometres southwest of Dantari Hill. With its advantageous location, the site

Fig. 6.6. Different types of megaliths at Shakteshgarh

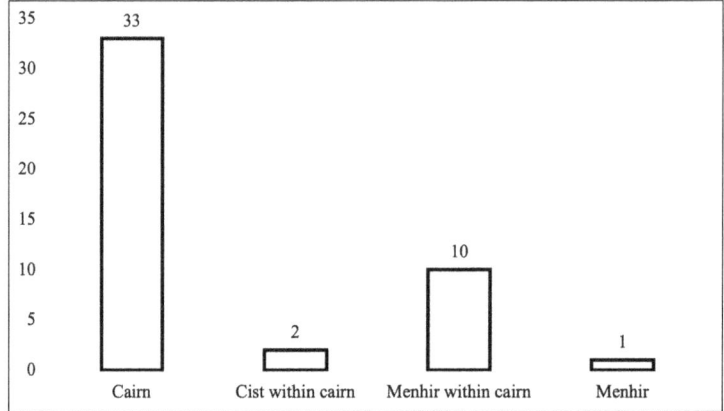

Fig. 6.7. Size variations of megalithic burials at Shakteshgarh

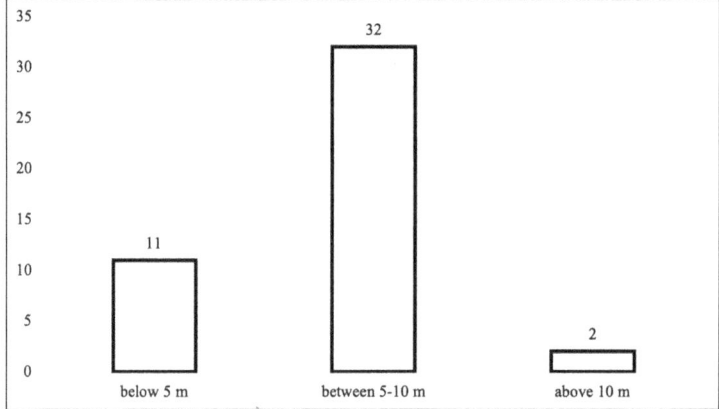

has access to multiple water sources, including the Pachbahani River, ensuring a reliable supply. Compared to other sites, the megalithic burials at Bahera have suffered more significant damage because of a local road running through the cemetery. Locals have taken dirt and stones from the megalithic deposit for personal use and treasure. Approximately 120 megalithic structures exist here, including cairns, cist within cairns, menhir within a cairn, and several independent menhirs (Fig. 6.8). The cairn appears to be the most popular type, as the majority of the megaliths at Bahera fall into this category. The size of the cairns varies, with circumferences ranging from 3 to 15 metres and an average height of 0.15 to 1.25 metres above the ground. Megaliths with diameters between 5 and 10 meters comprise the largest number (Fig. 6.9).

Siddhanath-Ki-Dari (24.96899, 82.82216)

The megalithic site of Siddhanath-Ki-Dari is situated approximately 25 km southwest of Chunar tehsil. It is marked solely by a cemetery that measures around 100 by 80 metres. Megalithic burials are primarily found on the slope of a hill. The site features only 12 cairn-

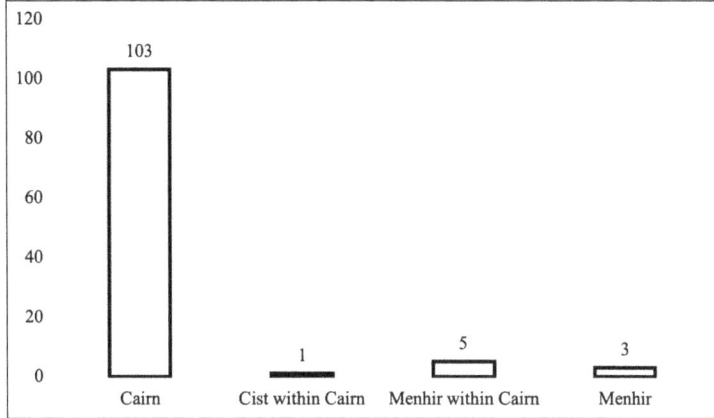

Fig.6.8. Different types of megaliths documented in Bahera

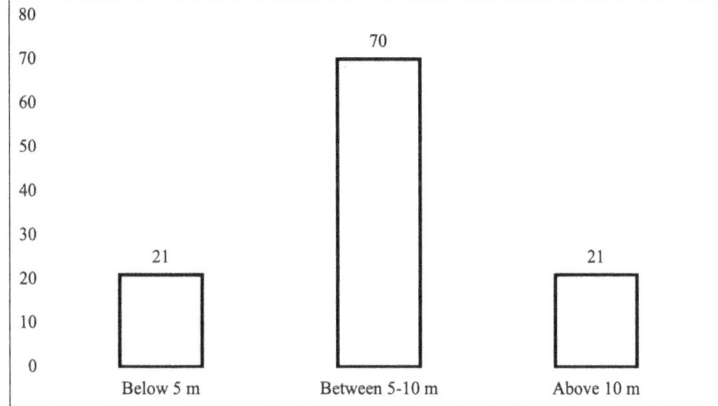

Fig. 6.9. Size variations of megaliths at Bahera

type burials (Fig. 6.10), with diameters ranging from 3 to 6 metres and an average height extending from 10 cm to 35 cm above the current surface. Most of the megaliths are in a disturbed condition.

Samudwa (25.01787, 82.85879)

A megalithic burial site, Samudwa located approximately 20 kilometres south of Chunar. The burials are located on the hill's desolate landscape, primarily on its slopes and centre. This place has yielded a total of 16 megalithic burials. Based on surface identification, cairns are likely the most common type of megalith (Fig. 6.11). The circumference of cairns ranged from 3 to 8 meters, with an average height above the existing surface of 10 to 65 centimetres (Fig. 6.12).

Rampur-38 (24.90267, 82.87464)

In the Mirzapur district, Rampur-38 is situated approximately 30 km southeast of Chunar. The megalithic burials at Rampur-38 are found on an uncultivated rocky outcrop. The burial cemetery comprises 32

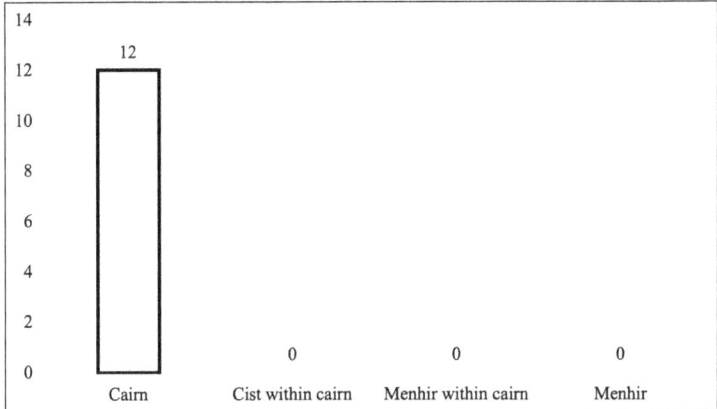

Fig. 6.10. Different types of megaliths at Siddhanath-Ki-Dari

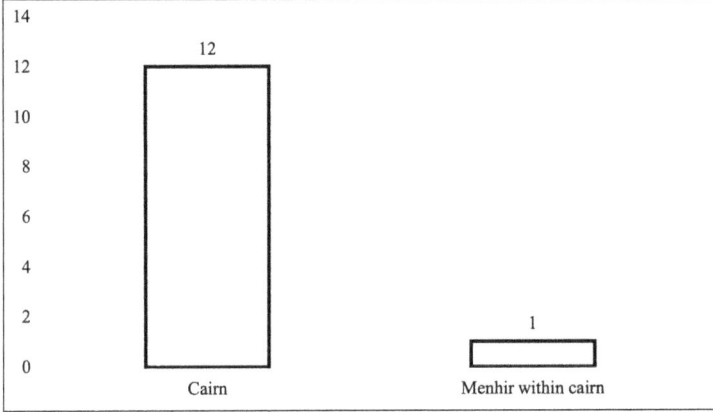

Fig.6.11. Different types of megaliths at Samudwa

megalithic burials of various types (Fig. 6.13). The most prevalent types are cairns and menhir within cairns. The diameters of the cairns range from 3 to 18 metres (Fig. 6.14). Several megaliths have been disturbed due stone quarries and human interference.

Siyanhara (25.04938, 82.90897)

Siyanhara site is located 13 kilometres east of Chunar Tehsil. Here, 30 megalithic burials are in a long row on both sides of Dhaunha-Jargo dam road. The cemetery comprises cairns and cist within cairns that range from 5 to 8 meters in diameter and an average height of 10 to 95 centimetres from the surface. Stone quarrying destroyed several megaliths at this location. Because of the dense vegetation, we could not document the burials.

Kharian Jangal-Mahal (25.04872, 82.93434)

This megalithic burial site is located near the Jargo dam, 18 kilometres east of Chunar Tehsil. Presently, the site contains only two intact

Archaeology of Chunar: Megaliths, Microliths and Rock Paintings

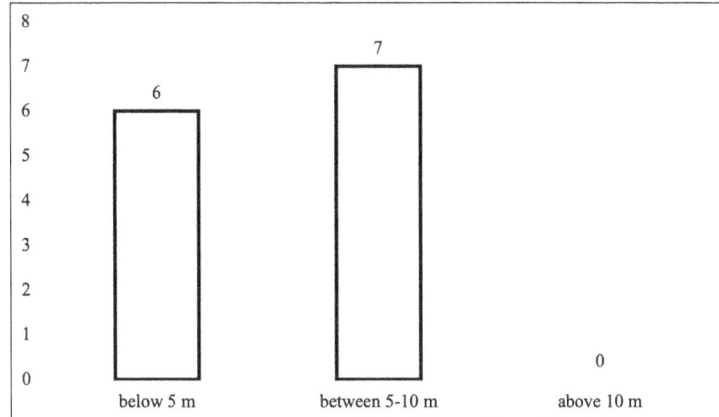

Fig. 6.12. Size variations of megaliths at Samudwa

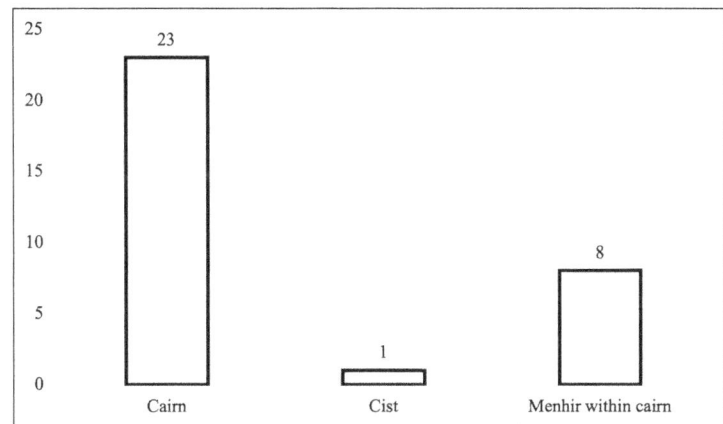

Fig. 6.13. Different types of megalithic burials at Rampur-38

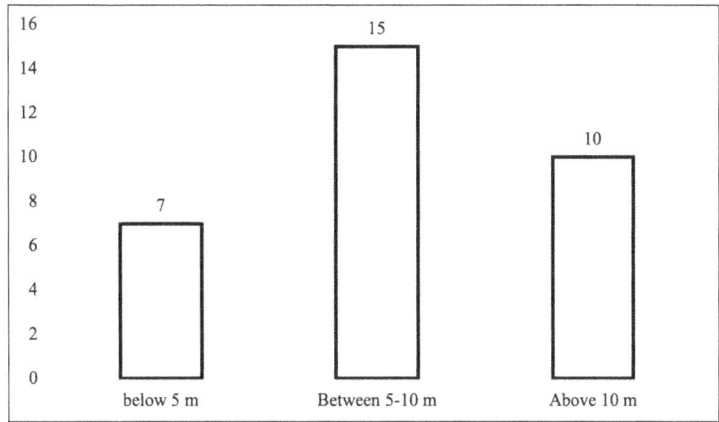

Fig. 6.14. Different sizes of megaliths at Rampur-38

cairn burials; however, it must have included sufficient megaliths in earlier times that have not survived today. The diameter of the two megaliths ranged between 3 and 5 meters, and their average height was between 17 and 22 centimetres from the present ground.

Kumhia (25.031088, 82.91288)

Kumhia is located 15 km southeast of Chunar tehsil of Mirzapur district. The burial site is also near to the Jargo Dam. The megaliths are situated on the barren terrain of the small hill and the slopes. Approximately 50 megalithic burials are identified here. Based on available structural details, the chief megaliths were probably cairns and cist within cairns. The circumference of burials varied from 3 to 15 m, and its average height above the present surface is ordinarily 10 to 65 cm. The megaliths have mostly been destroyed because of plundering, and only the outer sections can be seen. Residents transport the capstones from the megaliths to their homes, and one can observe contemporary buildings constructed over the cemetery. Due to the considerable vegetation, we could not document the site properly.

Talaiya (24.90672, 82.83319)

The megalithic burial site Talaiya is located on the left side of the Chunar-Rajgarh road. Approximately seven megalithic burials, most of which are cairns, are present at the site. The megaliths' average diameter was between 4 and 6 meters, and their average deposition was 10 to 20 cm.

Semri-Sarso (24.9365, 82.82287)

Semri-Sarso megalithic burial site is located near the Chunar-Sonbhadra railway track. It is situated 25 kilometres south of Chunar tehsil in the Mirzapur district. Presently, the site contains only four cairn burials; however, it must have contained numerous megaliths in earlier times. The diameter of the megaliths ranged between 5 and 7 meters and had an average height of 15 and 30 centimetres from the existing surface.

Pokhraudh (24.90318, 82.81504)

The megalithic site of Pokhraudh is located near the Rajgarh block, about 30 kilometres southwest of Chunar Tehsil in the Mirzapur district. It currently has only one cist megalith, but surface observation indicates that it might have had sufficient megaliths that have vanished once.

Painted Rock Shelters

The southern region of Chunar provides a perfect environment for painted rock shelters due to its geographical conditions. The landscape of this region consists of small hills and limited fertile land. These barren hills lack dense vegetation, and natural shelters are scarce because of their low elevation. As a result, evidence of human painting in this area is minimal. The painted rock shelters reported in this region are as follows:

Siddhanath-Ki-Dari (24.96397, 82.82153)

Siddhanath-Ki-Dari is located approximately 15 km southwest of Dantari Hill. Two painted rock shelters on the Jargo River's banks have been reported here. These shelters feature images of hunters, animals, and birds, all depicted using dark red pigment. Based on the style of the paintings and the presence of microliths found at the site, these rock shelters have been attributed to the Mesolithic period (Tewari 1997:51-58; 1999:163-223).

Pahati Dari (24.97670, 82.74063)

Pahati Dari is located approximately 17 km west of Dantari Hill. Five painted rock shelters have been identified at this site, situated along the banks of the Pahati River (Tewari 1997:51-58; 1990:163-223; 1999). These shelters feature images of hunters, animals, birds, humans, warriors, nature scenes, and geometric designs, all created using dark red and orange pigments. Most of these images are faded.

Nanauti Dari (24.97326, 82.78279)

Nanauti Dari, also known as Golhanpur ki Dari, is approximately 13 kilometres west of Dantari Hill. The painted rock shelter lies east of Nanauti Nala. The shelter contains images of hunters, animals, and birds, all created using dark red pigment. Some of these images are faded due to the long exposure. Several microlithic tools, made from chert, chalcedony, and agate materials, have also been recovered from the site (Tewari 1997:51-58).

Bairahawa (24.89955, 82.92784)

Bairahawa is located in the Jangal Mahal area of Chunar tehsil. A painted rock shelter depicting hunting scenes and domesticated animals has been discovered here. Based on style, the paintings in this shelter have been categorised into two groups. The first group consists of crude depictions made in dark brown, while the second group shows more developed and refined images created using ocher pigment. Microlithic tools from materials such as chert, chalcedony, and agate have been found at the site (Kumar 2022; IAR 1962-63: 35).

Gobardaha (25.00008, 82.84346)

Rock Shelter is located on the Chunar-Rajgarh road, approximately 6 km west of Dantari. A painted rock shelter has been discovered here on the banks of the Pachbahani River (Kumar 2022). The shelter measures 8 feet in width and 5 feet in height and is oriented facing south. Inside the shelter, two Alpana-shaped paintings have been created using ocher pigment. These paintings employ a single linear geometric style, featuring two concentric circles at the centre. Based on stylistic analysis, this shelter is considered a historical period dated between 300 CE and 700 CE (Tewari 1990).

Microlithic Sites

Microliths have been documented from various sites in the southern area of Chunar. These microliths are associated with megalithic and painted rock shelter sites; in some instances, they have been found independently. Microliths from Siddhanath-ki-Dari, Pahati Dari, Gobardaha, Nanauti Dari, and Bairahawa are associated with painted rock shelters and probably belong to the Mesolithic period (Tewari 1997:51-58; 1999:163-223; Kumar 2022). Microliths have been recovered from sites such as Maina Pahar, Kumhia, Bajahur, Sakteshgarh, Banbaira Pahar, Jaugarh, and Bahera, which are related to megalithic cemeteries. Evidence of independent microlith production workshops has been identified at sites including Gargaraha Nala, Churiharawa Nala, Jaugarh, Darhada Nala, Thekwah, Pansile Dari, Bhaluhi Pahadi, and Lalpur field (Tewari 1997:51-58). These sites have yielded tools such as blades, fluted cores, flakes, debitage, and chips made from chert, chalcedony, agate, jasper, and banded agate.

Habitation Sites

The discovery of three habitation sites near Dantari Hill provides evidence of human habitation. These sites are located in the villages near Dantari Hill called Baheri, Banimilia and Bahera (Fig. 6.15). A brief description of each site is given below:

Baheri (25.02013, 82.9056)

The site is situated along the right bank of the Pachbahani River, south of Dantari Hill. The habitation deposit extends 120 metres from east to west and 100 metres from north to south. The mound

Fig. 6.15. General view of habitation mound at Baheri

rises 8 metres on the northern side, sloping towards the river (Fig. 6.16). The uppermost cultural deposits have been disturbed due to ongoing agricultural activities. The current surface of the deposit features artefacts and remnants, such as ceramics, beads, and associated materials from past cultures. The predominant pottery found at Baheri is red ware (thick and durable), comprising various shapes of bowls and pots. The red ware retrieved from the deposit is akin to that from other megalithic sites in the Vindhya region. Based on these potsherds, it is inferred that Baheri was a significant site during the Megalithic period. The proximity to the vast cemetery sites of Dantari Hill and Maina Pahar suggests that the site's deposit indicates the dwelling place of megalithic builders.

Banimilia (25.00809, 82.9248)

Banimilia is another habitation site located approximately 2 km southeast of Dantari Hill. The settlement mound measures 260 meters east-west and 210 meters north-south. Currently, a road divides the mound into two parts: the southern part, occupied by village residents and the northern part, used as an agricultural field (Fig. 6.17).

Using a cross-transect method, the team surveyed 14 points from the centre to document the mound. Three points were taken from the

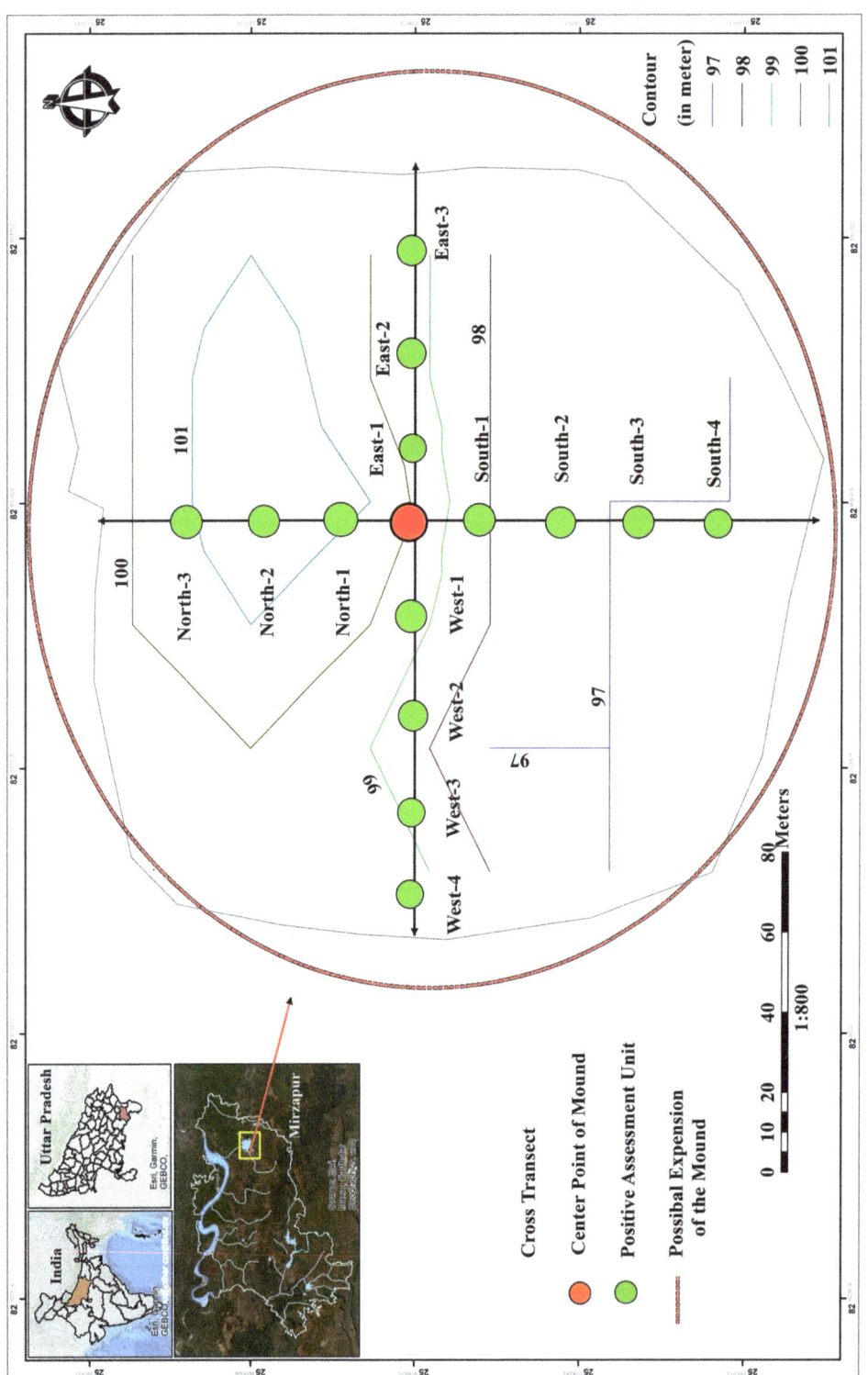

Fig. 6.16. Cross transect survey-layout of habitation mound at Baheri

Archaeology of Chunar: Megaliths, Microliths and Rock Paintings

Fig. 6.17. General view of habitation mound at Banimilia

east and west sides and four from the north and south sides. Each assessment point was placed 25 meters apart, and material remains were collected in separate bags from each end. Using GIS to generate a contour map, the mound's elevation was determined to be between 95 and 103 meters, resulting in a total elevation difference of 8 meters (Fig. 6.18).

After detailed documentation, different types of pottery were collected from the each point, including red ware, black-and-red ware, and black slipped ware (Fig. 6.19). Among the red ware, coarse red ware and red slipped ware are prominent. Within this category, the main shapes include vases with inverted and rounded rims, long-neck vases, pots, bowls, spouts, and storage jars. Based on the pottery, this mound indicates the cultural material from the Megalithic to the Gupta period. A broken human terracotta figure, a stone disc, and a fragment of glass objects have also been found (Fig. 6.20).

Bahera (25.01092, 82.89442)

Bahera is situated south of Dantari Hill, on the left bank of the Pachbahani River, about one km south of Bahera Village. It measures 110 meters from east to west and 120 meters from north to south. A major mound deposit has been disturbed due to agricultural activity and digging for soil (Fig. 6.21). Due to the disturbance of

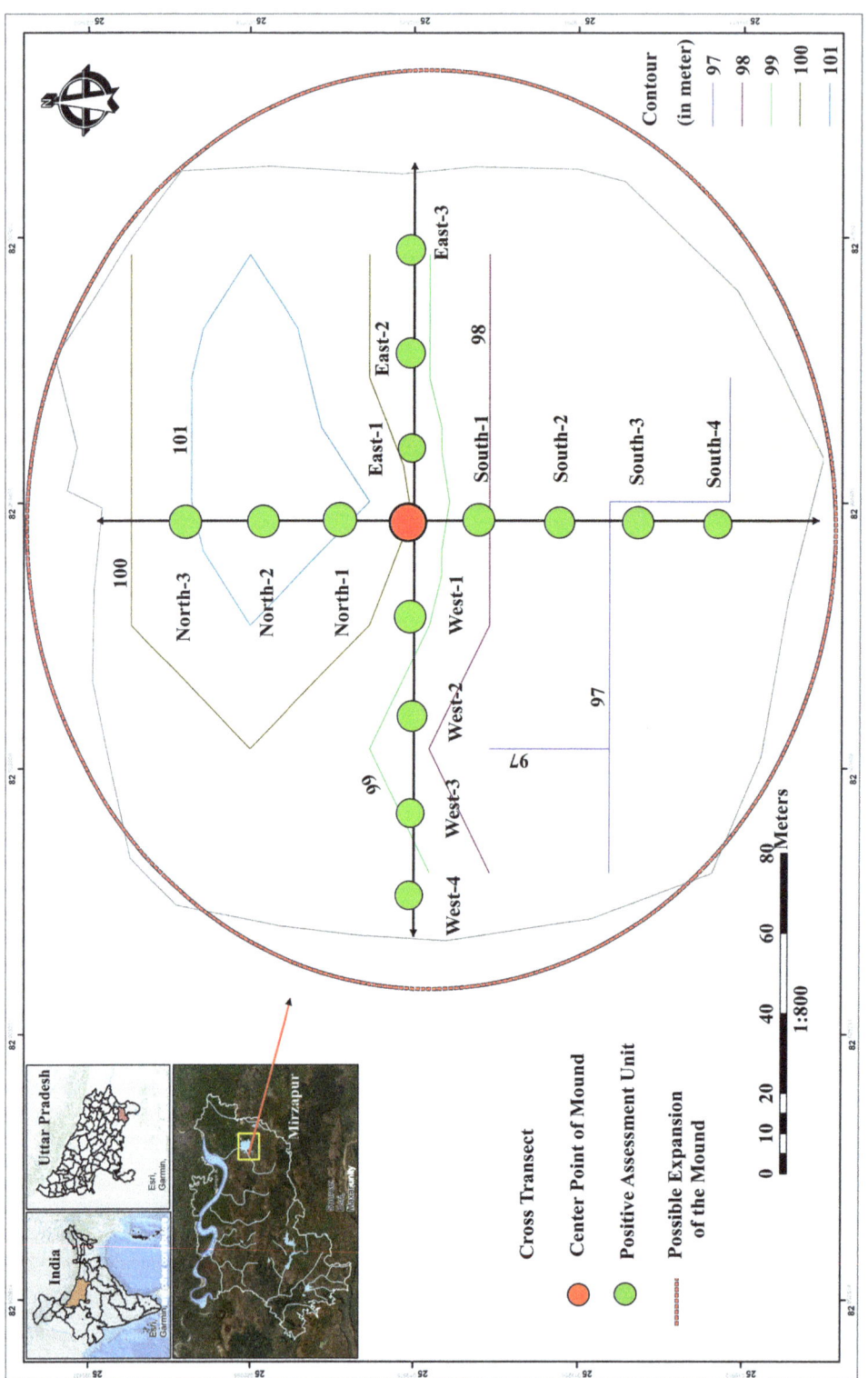

Fig. 6.18. Cross transect survey layout of habitation mound at Banimilia

Fig. 6.19. Potsherds recovered from habitation mound at Banimilia

the mound, material remains appeared on the surface. A significant number of potsherds are scattered on the surface. To understand the site's area, the micro documentation of the settlement was conducted using a cross-transect method. Eight points were taken at a distance of 25 meters from others in different directions. Using GIS to generate a contour map, an elevation of 5 meters was determined for this mound (Fig. 6.22). The pottery recovered from the ancient habitational deposit mainly comprises red ware and red slipped ware. The primary types include vases, bowls, sprinklers, pots, and storage jars (Fig. 6.23). Based on the pottery, this mound indicates the habitation of a Megalithic, Early Historical, and Kushana-Gupta period. The proximity to the megalithic cemetery area shows the megalithic habitation probably beneath the early historic deposit.

Fig. 6.20. Potsherds and associated findings recovered from habitation mound at Banimilia

Fig. 6.21. General view of habitation deposit at Bahera

Archaeology of Chunar: Megaliths, Microliths and Rock Paintings

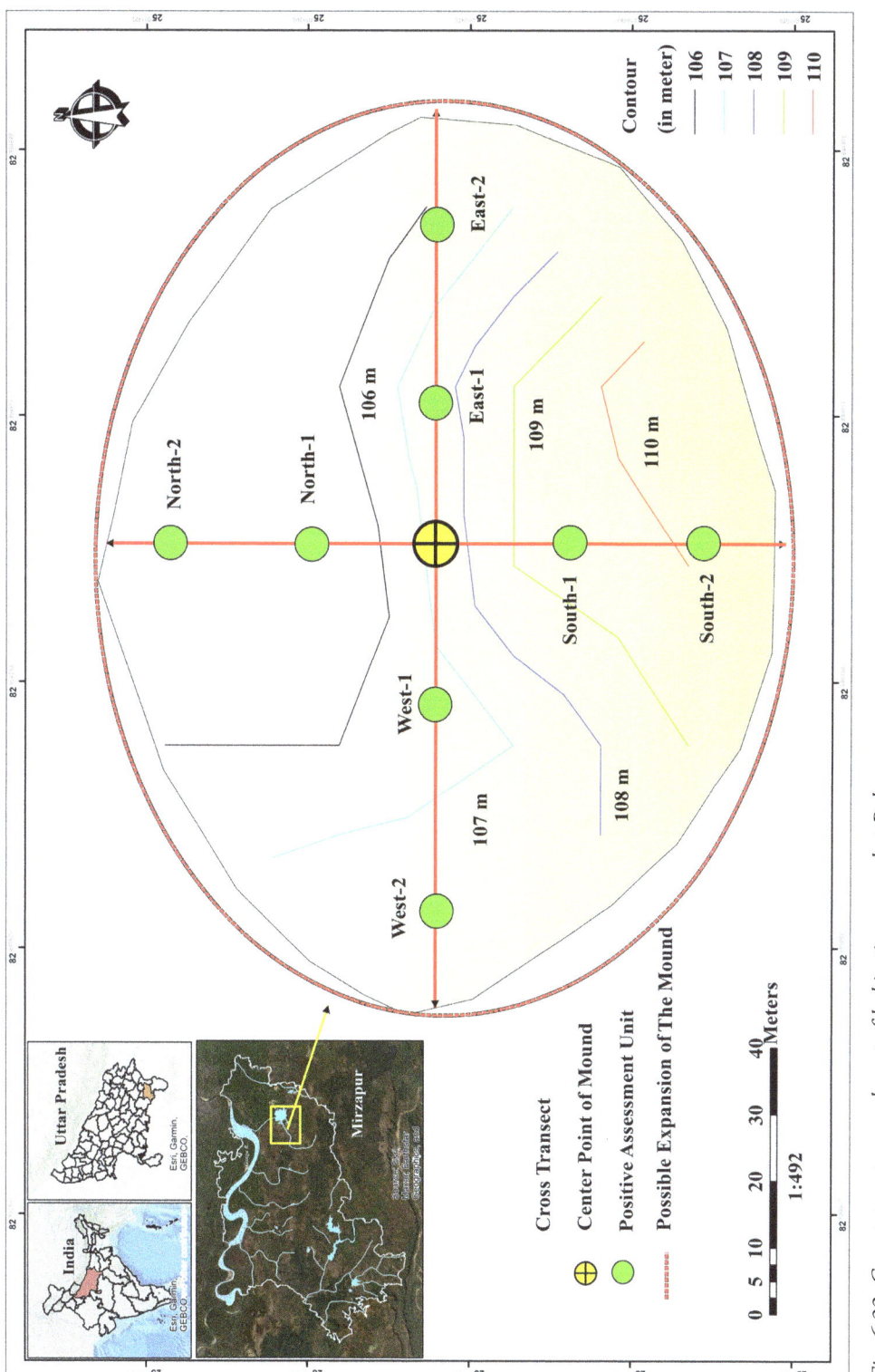

Fig. 6.22. Cross transect survey layout of habitation mound at Bahera

Pre and Protohistoric Archaeology of Chunar, Mirzapur (Uttar Pradesh)

Fig. 6.23. Potsherds recovered from habitation mound at Banimilia

Stone Quarry Sites

The southern part of Chunar is renowned for its rich sandstone resources, with evidence of extensive quarrying activity dating back to the Maurya period. Over 450 quarry sites were once active in this region, with Baragaon emerging as a significant centre for sandstone extraction (Pant and Jayaswal 1990: 49-52; Tewari 1999:163-223). Baragaon, located approximately 8 km north of Dantari on the banks of the Durga Nala, gained a reputation for producing many sandstone pillars. Many of these pillars remain scattered across the site today. The presence of inscriptions in Brahmi and Kharosthi script on certain pillars, dating back to the Mauryan and later periods, indicates the extensive history of sandstone quarrying in this region. A pillar from this site bears the name of a master craftsman from the Ashokan (Mauryan) period, inscribed in Kharosthi script. This discovery led to the hypothesis that Ashoka may have commissioned expert craftsmen from northwest India to carve pillars in this region (Pant and Jayaswal 1990: 49-52; Tewari 1999:163-223). Evidence suggests that these artisans played a significant role in constructing the iconic Mauryan pillars. Remarkably, stone quarrying continues in this area today, carried out by local communities, indicating a long-standing tradition of stone extraction in the region. The inscriptional record at Durga-Khoh in Chunar provides intriguing details about the rock-cutting workshop near the area. This inscription bears the names of 23 quarrymen or stone-cutters who were engaged in rock-cutting during the ancient period (Cunningham 1885:129). A similar inscription found on Dantari Hill provides further evidence of the names of rock-cutters. The inscription at Dantari appears to be written in a local dialect and the Kaithi script, recording names such as *Sumajha, Mamajha, Sadadajha,* and *Srinada*.

Discussion

The discovery of microliths at separate locations, such as the Chunar painted rock shelters and megalithic burials, suggests their widespread distribution across different cultures. This association indicates a broad distribution during various cultural periods. Similarly, the themes of the painted rock shelters offer valuable insights into their usage from prehistoric to historical times. Rock paintings and microliths are typically found on hillsides. The megalithic sites in this region are situated on small hills and plateaus within a barren landscape. Nearby rivers, fertile land, and diverse topography attracted settlers, prompting them to honour their burial rituals. The easy availability of stones, iron resources, diverse flora and fauna, plentiful water sources, vegetation cover, and alluvial zones have drawn humans since prehistoric times. Chakrabarti (1992) states that the Mirzapur district and its surroundings are well-known for their iron deposits, with magnetite being the primary ore found in bands. Megalithic burials are predominantly concentrated in low-elevation hills, with relatively fewer at higher elevations. Invariably, the megalithic cemeteries are located on a barren landscape, reflecting their ecological behaviour. The habitational sites are positioned near water sources and fertile alluvial areas. The cultural materials collected from these sites suggest occupation from the megalithic to the Gupta period. The inscription also indicates the enduring activity of stone quarrying throughout ancient India for various artistic and architectural purposes.

Chapter 7
Conclusion

Virag G. Sontakke. Sachin Kr. Tiwary and Dheeraj Sharma

According to recent archaeological investigations in the Chunar area of Mirzapur, humans have occupied this region since prehistoric times. The geographical locations and geophysical properties have been vital to the flourishing of various cultures in this area. The proximity of the River Ganga to the north and the majestic Vindhyan range to the south have made this area a suitable abode for ancient communities. Additionally, a natural rocky outcrop, barren landscapes, hills and ridges, lakes and rivers, diverse flora and fauna, and abundant resources bless this area, attracting settlers across different times and spaces.

The study of microlithic assemblages from Dantari Hill illuminates the technological and cultural practices of prehistoric communities in Central India. The site's rich collection of microliths, including blades, flakes, cores, and chips crafted from materials such as chert, chalcedony, agate, and quartz, highlights a well-developed lithic technology. The chapter on microliths systematically explores the significance of the Dantari microliths through an in-depth analysis of their collection methodologies, typology, spatial distribution, raw material usage, and production technology. The study reveals a significant level of sophistication in lithic technology, particularly in the production of microblades. Advanced knapping techniques, such as pressure flaking and indirect percussion, employed in creating microblades, demonstrate the prehistoric inhabitants' understanding of tool-making technology. Evidence of highly prepared platforms and strategic core reduction patterns underscores a systematic approach to maximising raw material use, highlighting cognitive sophistication and skills comparable to other microlithic traditions worldwide.

The association of microliths with megalithic burials and other archaeological contexts, such as rain gullies, slopes, and riverbeds, suggests that these tools played a multifaceted role within the prehistoric societies of Dantari Hill. Microliths as grave goods may signify symbolic or ceremonial importance, perhaps linked to status, ritual practices, or beliefs about the afterlife. The spatial distribution patterns identified within the 10 x 10 metre grid system at locality 4 provide crucial insights into the functional zoning of the site.

The concentration of microliths, particularly in mid-blocks D to H, indicates specialised activity areas dedicated to tool production. This evidence implies that Dantari Hill served as a factory site for lithic manufacturing and a significant cultural landscape for its inhabitants. The preference for chert over other materials, such as chalcedony, agate, and quartz, reveals a nuanced understanding of the properties of raw materials and their suitability for specific tool types. This choice also demonstrates the community's knowledge of local geological resources and their ability to optimise them for efficient tool production. Overall, the microlithic assemblage from Dantari Hill contributes substantial data to the broader context of microlithic cultures in Central India. It complements existing studies on sites such as Bhimbetka, Baghor, and Adamgarh, assisting in constructing a more comprehensive picture of prehistoric tool use, technological evolution, and cultural practices within this region. The variability in the sizes, shapes, and types of microliths from Dantari Hill mirrors the diversity observed in other Central Indian sites, offering a comparative framework for understanding regional adaptations and innovations.

This study is crucial in expanding our understanding of the microlithic culture in India, particularly within Central India. By examining Dantari Hill's microlithic assemblage through a detailed and systematic method, this study provides new insights into prehistoric communities' technological, cultural, and social aspects. The findings at Dantari Hill highlight the continuity of microlithic technology in the region and showcase distinctive local variations. This contributes to the ongoing debate about microlithic technology's origins, development, and spread across the Indian subcontinent. Dantari Hill's unique role as a production site and a burial ground sheds light on prehistoric settlement and land use patterns nuancedly. Various contexts reveal the presence of microliths, suggesting an intricate landscape where economic, social, and ritual activities were interconnected. The microlithic culture represents one of the longest cultural traditions in India, spanning from the Upper Paleolithic to the Mesolithic and into the Neolithic periods. The study of Dantari Hill's microliths contributes to the larger discourse on human adaptation, resilience, and technological innovation, which are key themes in the prehistory of the Indian subcontinent.

The microliths of Dantari Hill and its surroundings offer a comparative perspective on microlithic cultures within Central India. Like other well-known microlithic sites, the artefacts shared technological practices or cultural exchanges among prehistoric communities. The microliths discovered at Dantari Hill, similar to the assemblages at sites such as Kauva-khoh, Baghor II, and Adamgarh, are primarily composed of blades and micro-blades. The core reduction strategies, such as unidirectional flaking and platform preparation, share common technological approaches across these sites. Using chert as the primary raw material across different microlithic sites in Central India shows potential trade networks or shared knowledge about resource procurement. Non-local materials like agate and chalcedony also suggest interregional interactions or exchanges. The findings at Dantari Hill reflect the adaptability and continuity of microlithic traditions in response to changing environmental and socio-cultural contexts. This resonates with the broader patterns observed in Central India, where microlithic technology persisted and developed over millennia. The microlithic study of Dantari Hill offers valuable contributions to understanding the technological, cultural, and social dimensions of prehistoric communities in Central India. The research highlights the possibility of making further discoveries that could enhance our understanding of India's prehistoric history and the incredible resourcefulness of its ancient residents.

The rock art in Mirzapur is worth mentioning. Several sites located on the edges of the hill testimonials that the area was occupied during the Mesolithic period. Extensive examination has been conducted on the rock art of Dantari to comprehend its unique features and characteristics. The shelters' strategic connection to nearby water sources, shown by their southern orientation, suggests they may have functioned as a lookout point. A continuous human presence and activity over a long time is indicated by the variety of styles and subjects depicted in the pictographs at the site, suggesting its usage from the prehistoric era through the early medieval period. The abundant natural resources in and around Dantari were crucial in supporting prolonged human occupation. The discovery of numerous microliths in various rock types and forms postulates that the inhabitants extensively used diverse materials. The existence of the protohistoric period is highlighted by the prevalence of megalithic burials across its landscape. Dantari Hill, with one of the largest concentrations of megalithic graves attributed to the Vindhyan megalithic culture, highlights the site's enduring sacredness and importance across different eras and contexts.

In addition, Chunar is known for its numerous megalithic sites. It is noticed that the dominant megalithic sites are near river bodies and their fertile lands. Most sites in Mirzapur are concentrated in the alluvial tracts of the Ganga Valley and other river valleys, with hills and the Vindhyan plateau surrounding them. The area is rich in resources, especially those necessary to begin a settled culture. Stone, iron, flora and fauna, water, vegetation, and fertile alluvial soil were a few of the readily available factors on the Mirzapur site. Thus, compared to other nearby regions, this area was preferred by people back then. The Mesolithic period witnessed the intentional disposal of the dead for the first time. Sites like Lekhahia and Baghai Khor provided evidence of human burials in extended positions. This practice was followed in the megalithic period as well. Microliths also yielded from megalithic sites, which shows the continued relationship between both cultures.

In Chunar, megaliths are often situated close to water bodies, potentially showing their use as a primary water source (Fig. 7.1). The site also has access to small perennial to non-perennial river networks. Rivers like Jargo and Pachbahani also provide water to the region. Megaliths are usually seen as clusters, with each cluster comprising five to a maximum of thirty. There were also megaliths which are joined, which could be a sign of a family burial or burials of relatives or members of the same community. Ethnoarchaeological studies in Gond and Munda, tribes of central and eastern India, show similar customs where successive generations of the same family were buried together in a specific location (Elwin 1945; Geetali 2002:89-92; Shekhar et al. 2014).

Unquestionably, more effort and labour were required to erect the cist within the cairn, and their limited numbers reasonably suggest

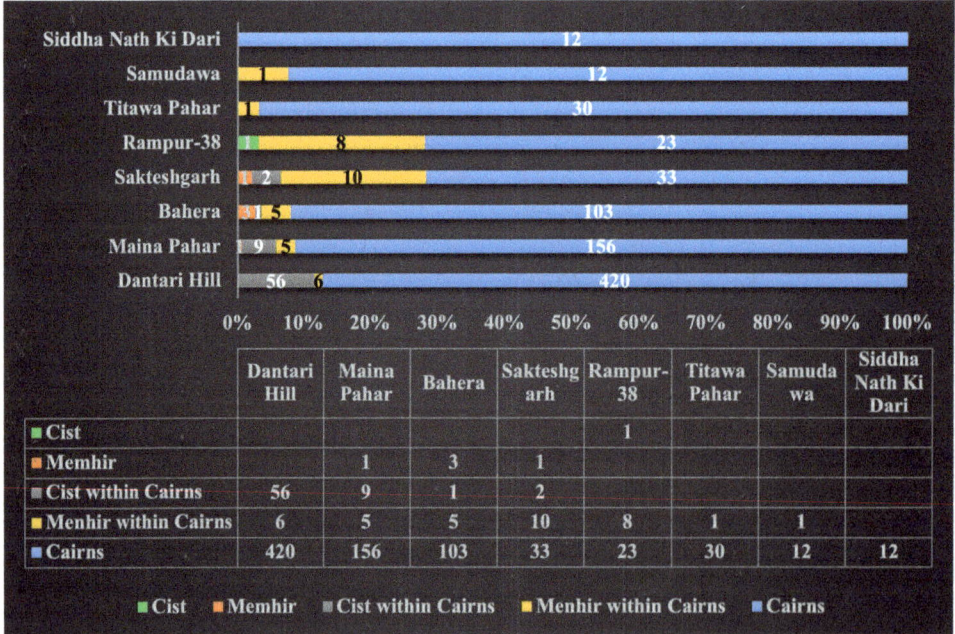

Fig. 7.1. Typological distribution of megaliths in Chunar, Mirzapur, Uttar Pradesh

	Dantari Hill	Maina Pahar	Bahera	Sakteshgarh	Rampur-38	Titawa Pahar	Samudawa	Siddha Nath Ki Dari
Cist				1				
Menhir		1	3	1				
Cist within Cairns	56	9	1	2				
Menhir within Cairns	6	5	5	10	8	1	1	
Cairns	420	156	103	33	23	30	12	12

that only a few specific people might afford this type of megalith. Socioeconomic hierarchy among the megalithic folk could also be identified in this scenario. Building large megaliths caused a larger workforce, typically involving the entire village and the deceased's relatives. Ethnoarchaeological research suggests that feasts played a crucial role in megalith construction. The erection of giant megaliths required more people and time, leading to multiple feasts, likely organised by individuals of higher socioeconomic status or those esteemed in the community (Elvin 1942, Mendaly 2015: 1-6). The high number of small megaliths suggests they were a popular choice, likely because they were more manageable for economically weaker groups. However, due to a lack of systematic research, the exact reasons for the differences in megalith sizes still need to be determined.

Usually, it is believed that the megaliths are located on the slope of hills as the availability of rocks will be higher. However, recent studies in the Chunar area show megaliths are found in almost all hill elevations from slop to the top. Megaliths at Chunar are located on an uncultivated barren land with a thin soil cover. The construction of megaliths was probably adjusted according to the characteristics of the surface. For example, a cairn with a cist is most likely present in areas where soil deposit is high, and cairns are found on natural bedrock.

Besides stones, iron was abundant in the surrounding areas. The iron deposits in Mirzapur, like magnetite found in sandstone of the Barakar age, exhibit characteristics similar to those of other locations. There is also an instance of yielding small nodules of hematite within the burial, which sheds light on the importance of hematite in that society. Iron might have been extracted and smelted on a large scale by megalithic people. Until recently, certain tribes like Agarias were engaged in iron manufacturing activity in Mirzapur. They mainly used rough ore, and the colour ranges from dusky red. Usually, the whole process takes about six to eight hours, with nearly every family member participating in it. The iron from Agaria is known for its high tenacity and endurance. It was also sold annually in the Ahraura market (Brockman 1911:25). From this analysis, it can be concluded that the iron at Mirzapur was smelted, manufactured and exchanged or traded with nearby sites in Gangetic zones. Recent evidence from sites such as Malhar and Raja Nal-ka-tila has pushed back the date of iron manufacturing in large quantities to the early second millennium BCE.

Megaliths are frequently discovered alongside water sources on Chunar, showing the significance of water in burial rituals. Cairns, cist within cairns, and menhirs within cairns are the main megalithic types observed in the area. Cairns are the most popular and often found in all cemetery sites. The cist within the cairn is the second most famous type found in Dantari. There are fewer menhirs within the area's cairns than previous types. The presence of menhirs in the Vindhya region contrasts with their wide existence in Chhattisgarh, which suggests potential cultural ties between these regions (Sontakke 2022: 39-51). Over centuries, nearly 500 megaliths at Dantari Hill show significant and sustained human activity. This site likely served as an important burial ground for the megalithic community of Mirzapur, highlighting its cultural and ritual significance.

The study of microliths, rock art, megaliths, and ceramics helps outline the tentative chronology of the area. Microliths and rock paintings suggest the area was first occupied, probably during the Mesolithic era. Non-geometric microliths made from chert, agate, and chalcedony highlight this phase. Depictions of horse riders, bows, arrows, and spearheads in rock art indicate iron-using people responsible for the megalithic monuments during the proto-historic period. Rock art featuring warriors and weaponry reflects the sociological changes of the early historic period. Ceramics and Nagari script inscriptions on a boulder near a water source suggest continuous occupation up to the early medieval period, enriching our understanding of the region's historical continuity.

Bibliography

Average Rain Fall Data. (2024). Center for Hydrometeorology and Remote Sensing. https://chrs.web.uci.edu

Balter, M. (2010). Of two minds about toba's impact. In *Science* (Vol. 327, Issue 5970, pp. 1187–1188). https://doi.org/10.1126/science.327.5970.1187-a

Bhukosh. (2024). *Geology 2M (Shape File Data)*. Geological Survey of India. https://bhukosh.gsi.gov.in/Bhukosh/MapViewer.aspx

Brockman, D. D. L. (1911). *Mirzapur: A Gazetteer* (Vol. 27). Allahabad: Superintendent Government Press.

Carlleyle, A. C. (1883). Notes on Lately Discovered Sepulchral Mound, Cairns, Caves, Cave Paintings, and Stone Implements. *Proceedings of the Asiatic Society of Bengal*: 49–55.

Chakrabarti, D. K. (1992). *The Early Use of Iron in India*. New Delhi: Oxford University Press.

Clark, J. D. (1985). The Microlithic Industries of Africa: Their Antiquity and Possible Economic Implications. *Recent Advances in Indo-Pacific Prehistory*: 95–103. New Delhi: IBH Publisher.

Cockburn, J. (1883a). A Short Account of the Petrographs in the Caves or Rock Shelters in the Kaimur Range in the Mirzapur District. *Proceedings of the Asiatic Society of Bengal*: 125–126.

Cockburn, J. (1883b). On the Recent Existence of the Rhinoceros Indicus in the North Western Provinces, and a Description of a Tracing of an Archaic Painting from Mirzapore Representing the Hunting of This Animal. *Journal of the Asiatic Society of Bengal, 52*(2), 56–64.

Cockburn, J. (1884a). On the Durability of Haematite Drawings on Sandstone Rocks. *Proceeding of the Asiatic Society of Bengal*, 141–143.

Cockburn, J. (1884b). On the Recent Extinction of a Species of Rhinoceros in the Rajmahal Hills and Bos Gaurus in the Mirzapur District. *Proceeding of the Asiatic Society of Bengal*, 140–141.

Cockburn, J. (1888). On Palaeolithic Implements from the Drift Gravels of the Singrauli Basin, South Mirzapore. *The Journal of the Anthropological Institute of Great Britain and Ireland* Vol. 17, 57–65. https://about.jstor.org/terms

Cockburn, J. (1889). Cave Drawing in the Kaimur Range, North Western Provinces. *Journal of the Royal Asiatic Society*, 89–97.

Cunningham, A. (1871). *Archaeological Survey Of India* (Vol. 1). Calcutta: Government Central Press.

Cunningham, A. (1885). *A Tour in Rewa, Bundelkhand, Malwa, and, Gwalior in 1884-85*. Calcutta: The Superintendent of Government Printing Press.

Elwin, V. (1942). *The Agaria*. Calcutta: Oxford University Press.

Elwin, V. (1945). *Funerary Customs In Bastar State* (Vol. 25). Man In India.

Geetali, A. (2002). Living Megalithic Practices Among the Madia Gonds of Bhamragad, District Gadchiroli, Maharashtra. *Puratattva* 32, 89–92.

Ghosh, M. (1932). Rock Paintings and Other Antiquities of Prehistoric and Later Times. *Memoirs of the Archaeological Survey of India*, 24, 14–19.

Henwood, W. J. (1856). Megalithic Culture of Devidhora in Almora. *Edinburgh New Philosophical Journal, New Series*, 204–205.

Herbert, A. (1849). *A Cyclops Christianus, or The Supposed Antiquity of Stonehenge and Other Megalithic Erections in Englang and Britanny*. London: John Petheram.

Indian Archaeology 1956-57- A Review. Archaeological Survey of India: New Delhi, 11–14.

Indian Archaeology 1962-63- A Review. Archaeological Survey of India: New Delhi, 31–32; 35; 37; 38–39; 39–41.

Indian Archaeology 1963-64- A Review. Archaeological Survey of India: New Delhi, 39; 51–52.

Indian Archaeology 1969-70- A Review. Archaeological Survey of India: New Delhi, 36–38.

Indian Archaeology 1975-76- A Review. Archaeological Survey of India: New Delhi, 43–44.

Indian Archaeology 1977-78- A Review. Archaeological Survey of India: New Delhi, 56–58.

Indian Archaeology 1990-91- A Review. Archaeological Survey of India: New Delhi, 75.

Jayaswal, Vidula (1998). *From Stone Quarry to Sculpturing Workshop : A Report on the Archaeological Investigations around Chunar, Varanasi & Sarnath*. Delhi: Agam Kala Prakashan.

Kaur, Singh, G., S., Kaur, P., Garg, S., Fareeduddin, Pandit, M. K., Agrawal, P., Acharya, K., & Ahuja, A. (2019). Vindhyan Sandstone: a Crowning Glory of Architectonic Heritage from India. *Geoheritage*, *11*(4), 1771–1783. https://doi.org/10.1007/s12371-019-00389-8

Kumar, M. (2022). *Mirzapur Ka Puratattva (in Hindi)*. New Delhi: Swati Publication.

Le Mesurier, H. P. (1867). Cairn. In *Proceedings of the Asiatic Society of Bengal: Vol. January* (pp. 164–166). Baptist Mission Press.

Mathpal, Y. 1984. Prehistoric Rock Paintings of Central India. New Delhi: Abhinav Publication.

Mendaly, S. (2015). A Study of Living Megalithic Tradition Among the Gond Tribes, District – Nuaparha, Odisha. *Ancient Asia*, *6*(9), 1–6. https://doi.org/10.5334/aa.12328

Misra, V. D., Misra, B. B., Pal, J. N., Gupta, M. C., & Kumar, A. (2014). The Megalithic culture of Adwa valley in North Central Vindhyas. K. N. Dikshit & A. Kumar (Eds.), *The Megalithic Culture of South India* (Vol. 6, pp. 342–375). New Delhi: The Indian Archaeological Society.

Misra, V. N. (2001). Prehistoric Human Colonization of India. *Journal of Biosciences*, *26*, 491–531.

Neumayer, E. (2013). *Prehistoric Rock Art of India*. Delhi: Oxford University Press.

Pant, P. C. (1985). The Megaliths of Jangal Mahal, and Vedic Tradition. V. N. Misra & P. Bellwood (Eds.), *Recent Advances in Indo-Pacific Prehistory* (pp. 481–484). New Delhi: Oxford & IBH Publishing Co.

Pant, P. C., & Jayaswal, V. (1990). Ancient Stone Quarries of Chunar. *Pragdhara*, *1*, 49–52.

Pratap, A. (2016). *Rock Art of the Vindhyas: An Archaeological Survey: Documentation and Analysis of the Rock Art of Mirzapur District, Uttar Pradesh*. Oxford: Archaeopress.

Pratap, A. (2024). *Idea and Images: A Historical Interpretation of Eastern Vindhyan Rock Art, India*. Oxford: Archaeopress.

Shekhar, H., Pawar, K., & Jun, K. Y. (2014). Living Megalithic Tradition Amongst the Munda Community of Jharkhand. *Heritage: Journal of Multidisciplinary Studies in Archaeology 2*, *2*, 705–719.

Singh, P., & Singh, A. K. (2004). *The Archaeology of Middle Ganga Plain* (Vol. 1). New Delhi: Aryan Books International.

Singh, A.K. & Ravi Shankar (2018). Ceramic Industry of Agiabir, Dist. Mirzapur: A Study, *Bharati*, 41, 95-129.

Sontakke, Virag. (2022). Megalithic Culture of Vidarbha, Maharashtra: Inter-regional Relationships, *Puratattva*, 52, 39-51.

Tewari, R. (1990). *Rock Paintings of Mirzapur*. Lucknow: Eureka Printers.

Tewari, R. (1997). Gram Stariya Sarvekshan: Vikaskhand- Rajgarh: Jila- Mirzapur (Hindi). R. Tewari (Ed.), *Pragdhara* 7: 51–58).

Tewari, R. (1999). Archaeological Investigation in Mirzapur. *Pragdhara*, 9, 163–223.

Tiwary, S. K. (2013). Decoding Death: Connotation of the Cross in the Circle in Indian Rock Art. *Valcamonica Symposium*, 25, 381–388.

Tixier, J. (1963). *Typologie de L'epipaleolithique du Maghreb*. France: Arts et Metiers Graphiques.

Varma, R. K. (1984). The Rock Art of Southern Uttar Pradesh with Special References to Mirzapur. *Rock Art of India*, 206–213.

Varma, R.K. (1986). *The Mesolithic Age in Mirzapur*. Allahabad: Paramjyoti Prakashan.

Varma, R.K. (2012). *Rock Art of Central India: North Vindhyan Region*. New Delhi: Aryan Book International.

www.ingramcontent.com/pod-product-compliance
Lightning Source LLC
Chambersburg PA
CBHW061936290426
44113CB00025B/2927